The Spirituality of

ST. IGNATIUS LOYOLA

LOYOLA UNIVERSITY PRESS
is pleased to make
this out-of-print book
available once again
to its old friends.

This book* is a

Loyola

request

reprint

*Reprinted by arrangement with the author
and/or the original publisher.
This book is now sold only by
Loyola University Press.

The Spirituality

OF

ST. IGNATIUS LOYOLA

An Account of Its Historical Development

by HUGO RAHNER, S.J.

Translated by
FRANCIS JOHN SMITH, S.J.

LOYOLA UNIVERSITY PRESS
Chicago 60657

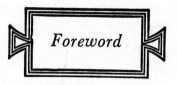

Foreword

THE ultimate purpose and the subject matter of this book call for a word of explanation, since at first sight the two seem to have little or no connection with each other.

The final aim of the book may be stated in a single phrase: service in the Church. The word "service" is a sacred word and conceals within itself a whole hierarchy of values, which rise one above the other to the highest within reach of a rational creature, the service of God. The word itself as well as those who are willing to render service has been misused in order to train slaves of the state. As a consequence there is a newly awakened sensitivity which makes many unwilling to hear even the word "service." For them it is synonymous with a helpless, galling servility or a task performed without love. Today we must restore the sacredness of service by showing that there still exists one kingdom—and only one—in which a man can render service as a free and joyous servant, as a noble soldier. This is the Kingdom of God, existing here in the Church. There is all the more necessity for proclaiming this fact because voices of unfavorable criticism have been raised in the very portals of the

Church. True, this criticism is often "nothing more than the indignation and complaints of love" (Ida Friederike Görres), and proceeds from a highly sensitive love for the Mystical Body of Christ, the Church. But it is impossible to eliminate safely the danger of a new form of spirituality unless one proves its genuineness and justifiableness by sober, humble service in the Church. It is just this commonplaceness which is the Church's most hidden and Christian mystery.

The aim of this book is to serve as interpreter of those profound words of our Holy Father, Pope Pius XII, in his encyclical on the Mystical Body of Christ: "It is not enough to love this Body for the glory of its Divine Head and its members who are in heaven. We must also manifest love by deeds toward those still in this mortal life." Since the days of St. Ignatius, this attitude has been called "thinking with the Church"; for this true servant, this noble soldier of the Church, was the one who handed down to us these "Rules for Thinking Rightly with the Church." This attitude is as old as the Church herself. Accordingly, it is the purpose of our book to present the development of the essential features and history of this spirit of service in the Church.

What has been said will serve as a justification for the apparently remote connection between the subject matter of the book and its purpose. Speculative consideration tends to become more questionable, the more sublime and incomprehensible "the attitude" we have to circumscribe and fix within bounds. To ward off this danger we must keep before our minds the realization of this attitude which can be seen only in man as he actually appears in history. We come to know what is saintly only through the saints. Hence we choose a saint whose ideal of perfection is essentially formed by service in the Church, namely, St. Ignatius Loyola. All results of our studies in the life of this Saint may seem at first blush to refer only to the narrower field of the history of the Society of Jesus, but we shall use them to serve our ultimate aim as fixed above. However, it is only by this historical fidelity to smaller things that we shall be able to raise and extend our gaze across the undiscovered and immense lands of the mysterious history of the spirit where the great men of the Church from Ignatius of Antioch onward join hands with one another. These men transmit from generation to generation that loyalty to the humble Church here on earth which is so needed by the men of our day. They have been cruelly disillusioned by all worldly slogans and passionately long for an ideal as a model of their lives.

If this book can contribute, even in a small way, toward exciting in the hearts of the present generation of Christians a willingness to serve in the Church such as we see exemplified in the lives of her great men at all times—a willingness to serve that is modest in speech and criticism, but courageously energetic in action—then it has accomplished its purpose.

HUGO RAHNER, S.J.

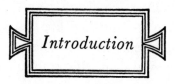

Introduction

I<small>T IS THE</small> unanimous opinion of both friends and enemies of the Society of Jesus that St. Ignatius was instrumental, by means of his Spiritual Exercises and by the Order he founded, in turning the course of Church history into new channels. "Since the dawn of history," says R. Fülop-Miller, "there are few men who have followed out an idea to its bitter end with such iron logic, few men who have realized it with such an extraordinary output of energy and exerted such a profound influence upon the thought and action of mankind as Ignatius did." It is in this sense that his Spiritual Exercises are praised "as a book of destiny for mankind" (H. Böhmer), and his Order is conceded the glory of having done great work for civilization. This concession is made by J. C. Herder, for instance, in his *Adrastea:* "Though the name, *Jesuit,* would remain odious in all other respects, yet the good the Order has done for the human race will always be worthy of praise and will undoubtedly continue to be profitable for future generations."

These critical views, however, touch only the surface of history. Ignatius and his lifework are understood only by those who delve deep into the hidden depths where the gigantic forces of his life's achievement are released by his secret wrestlings with God. In the final analysis, the influence of Ignatius and his Order upon the Church, upon politics, civilization and world-wide missions, derives from the spiritual life that animated them. For the great achievements which history records always have their beginnings in the tranquil center of the human heart.

Therefore we shall boldly attempt to lay bare in this study the history of the underlying forces of that ideal which St. Ignatius wished to exemplify in his own life and to bequeath to his Order.

But the attempt to uncover the history-making forces that build up the body of Christ—edification in the deepest sense of the word—demands justification both in content and in method. As to method, the question immediately arises: Is it possible at all to have a history of the human heart and its mysterious encounters with God? If the writing of history is to remain what it ought to be, then it must adhere to the sources with exactness; but the human heart is forever beyond all earthly witnesses. We desire to write both history and the unwitnessed secrets of the heart. It is indeed a bold undertaking to seek to penetrate beneath the surface of the documented sources to relive the way the Christian heart draws from the living spring that force of whose effects we may read in casually written accounts. But such an attempt is of the utmost importance for deepening our knowledge of history. This we shall endeavor to do for Ignatius and his lifework, for his Spiritual Exercises, and for the ideal of perfection bequeathed by Ignatius to the Society he

founded. Our attempt will be based on as accurate a
knowledge of the sources as possible, for otherwise our
work would descend to the level of a merely edifying tale
or an unwarranted psychological romance. However, by
breaking through the surface of texts in the sources, we
aim at reaching those depths which lie beyond the pale
of pure history, where the countenance of St. Ignatius in
his contemplation of God takes on those unforgettable
lineaments which he has handed down in the books of
his spiritual experiences and in the books of the foundation of his Order. For otherwise we would remain tied
down to the purely superficial type of history that merely
arranges and chronicles facts and has no rule either for
praise or blame by which to measure the world-trans-
forming figure of Loyola.

As to content, our attempt is justified by the following considerations: It is a long-established fact of history
that the character and thought of Ignatius found their
clearest expression in the book of Spiritual Exercises and
that his Order arose and is ever freshly renewed from
that world of thought. But beneath the sparse words of
the book of Exercises and the close-clipped sentences
of the Constitutions there lies hidden a whole new world:
the world of the heart of Ignatius—a clear world, yet
at the same time a glowing world, one which Ignatius
created from those few blinding illuminations received by
him at Manresa during his mystical encounter with God.
It is our desire to push forward into this world in order
to get from it some inkling of the forces with which
Ignatius imbued his world-wide activity. We are concerned for the present, then, with determining the exact

starting point for our investigation into the history of the
Ignatian ideal.

That starting point is given by the fundamental truths
of the book of the Spiritual Exercises; they enable us to
enter into the very center of Ignatius' heart. According
to Ignatius' opinion, the Spiritual Exercises are not a
fully elaborated treatise on Christian perfection, but
merely an outline, a "principle and foundation" for the
life-transforming meeting of the soul with God. From
the two most important meditations of this book, the exercises of the Kingdom of Christ and of the Two Standards, it is possible to sum up in a single sentence the basic
plan for the formation of a life of perfection: Man is
created to fight in the Church militant against Satan by
reverent service of the majesty of the Triune God, by
making himself like to the crucified Jesus, and by so do-
ing to enter into the glory of the Father. The fundamental driving-force in all this is love: love that is
characterized by a word distinctive of Ignatius' whole
nature, the word "more" (*magis*); love which wants to
do ever "more and more," which is essentially limitless,
always open as it were to promptness in the service of
God and in its willingness to become like to Christ; love,
finally, which finds its measure in the immensity of the
Eternal Father's redeeming love made visible in the Incarnate Christ, love "desiring and choosing only those
things which lead more to the end for which I am
created."

The final step in the development of this love is an
element that is of decisive importance for a full understanding of the deep nature of Ignatius' thought. The

essential illimitability of the love driven on by the "more" is restricted by the ideal of service in the visible Church militant. This immeasurable love has to prove its genuine Catholicity by the measure, so to speak, of the flesh and blood of Christ's Mystical Body. In this way, boundless love becomes for Ignatius "discreet" love, to make use once again of one of Ignatius' key words. Every grace must be measured by the law of the Church; every love, by the spirit of obedience; every spirit, by the Mystical Body of Christ, our Lord. From the union of this irrepressible love with its limitations within the body of the Church is released that enormous force which can be verified historically in the work of St. Ignatius. That was the peculiar grace of Ignatius; in it lay hidden the deepest element of his ideal of perfection. "Not to be stopped by what is greatest, yet to be held in check by what is least, that is divine." This is the description given of the real Ignatius in the *Imago Primi Saeculi Societatis Jesu* (*1640*), written by an anonymous Jesuit. Hölderlin, as we know, greatly admired this line and placed it at the head of his work, *Hyperion*. This is the very essence of the spirit of Ignatius. He is the man of great love in the little Church.

As a consequence of this, our historical study extends its scope to an endeavor that seeks to fit the ideal of Ignatius and his Order into the general history of the development of perfection. It was precisely because he wished to place his unshackled love into the fetters of humble service in the Church, that he was changed to the little servant in the great Church. This conversion proves the genuineness of his ideal of perfection. The law stated above, namely, that every spirit must prove its genuineness by the law of the Church, holds true also as an historical law in the history of asceticism. There is no perfection which is not "incarnate spirit," if we may be allowed this expression. Even the apparently most sublime urging of the "more" of a spirit, if it refuses to fit itself into the humble body of the visible Church, ends up as a rule in a proud spirituality. The gnosticism of the early days of Christianity, the excesses of the Egyptian type of monasticism, the Origenism of oriental theology and the wild mysticism of the Friends of God in the Middle Ages—all bear out the truth of this statement. To offset such unrestrained luxuriance the Holy Spirit is always active, but only within the limits of the Church; just as He came down in His fullness, but only upon the flesh of the Incarnate Word, so He raised up chosen men of the Church who were to be living models of true perfection. Among this group of chosen men St. Ignatius is now also to be ranked. Accordingly, we shall attempt to disclose the relations existing between these men—relations which, independent of all historical contacts, have their roots in the deep bosom of God. We should like to trace out a history of the meta-historical disposition, so to speak, which with Ignatius we shall call "thinking rightly with the Church." Ignatius is here to be elevated to the ranks of the great men of the Church, men who safeguarded for the Mystical Body of Christ its spirit by keeping it within the bounds of the humble Church on earth.

But such an outward manifestation of the Church's ideal of perfection never finds its realization except in men as they actually exist. Hence it is to be gleaned in its outlines as well as in its conditions from the historical evolution of the man who is its prototype. That holds true also with regard to St. Ignatius. Consequently, our investigation must return again to the world of his spiritual development, though we must never lose sight of the purpose of the history of the inner heart of man as described above. This world can be known with historical exactness. It is one in which only a knowledge of the rich source materials can offer us safe guidance.

With the aid of these sources we may approach the subject of the inmost heart of Ignatius and see from three different angles the ideal he made live in the Exercises and in his Order. These three viewpoints will serve as a division of this study.

We approach first, as it were, from below—that is, we must inquire what influence his origin and descent, his education and attitude toward life, exerted upon the shaping of his basic ideas.

Secondly, we approach from the sides—that is, we must show how this fully molded personality was led into the world of the saints under the influence of Christian tradition.

Finally, we must approach from above—that is, we must explain how mystical grace took possession of his soul and transformed him with irresistible force into the man of the Church whose influence is still active even at the present day.

Contents

Contents

The Influence of Ignatius' Surroundings
Upon His Spiritual Formation

As HAPPENS in the case of every manifestation of true
life in the Church, the flame of a newly conceived ideal
of Christian perfection is kindled in the souls of those
who are called to it, amidst human conditions arranged
by Providence guiding the Church. It never rises in the
rarefied and chilly atmosphere of the purely intellectual,
but in such conditions of race and ancestry, of environment and education, that they become the starting point
which determines the character of the new ideal. They
exert a positive influence and often also a negative one.
But they always leave behind them permanent traces in
the total picture of this ideal of perfection. This picture
will always betray the peculiar form that a man of this
particular kind of origin has given it. Just as it is impossible, for example, to get a total picture of Augustine's
theology and spirituality without at the same time including the story of his sinful youth with all its experiences of concupiscence and Manichaean contempt of the

1

body; so also, the fine, late-Greek family culture of a great Cappadocian house in which St. Basil was reared, the bearing of Roman provincial nobility peculiar to St. Benedict, the hot Umbrian blood coursing through the veins of St. Francis of Assisi, the charm and elegance of French humanism that distinguished St. Francis de Sales—can never be wholly eradicated from the ideals of perfection formed by these men.

This holds true also for the ideal of perfection of the man who in the world bore the proud title Don Inigo Lopez de Loyola and later founded a company for the Church of his King.

1. Ignatius' Ancestry

Inigo Lopez de Loyola was descended from a noble Basque family which documents trace back to 1180, showing a record of unbroken loyalty in the service of the kings of Castile, the *Rey Catolico,* since the year 1200 (the year of the final separation of Guipuscoa from Navarre and of its union with Castile). The Loyolas were among the ten great families called *Parientes mayores;* they had the vested right of invitation to the king's court on certain occasions. Hence they felt that they really belonged to the court and the highest nobility, and therefore believed they were entitled from time to time to rebel against their king. It was owing to such self-willed rebellion that Inigo's grandfather was compelled to raze the tower that rose defiantly over Loyola castle and replace it by a less formidable structure. But such occasional acts of defiance were no argument against their constitutional loyalty. Inigo's father fought side by side with his king in the battle against the Moors before Granada. The sources speak of him as "a noble knight and great soldier." [1] Inigo's oldest brother fell in the expedition against Naples (1496); a second brother, named Hernandez, in the conquest of Mexico; a third, whose name is unknown, in the battle against the Turks in Hungary.[2] Father Nadal was right when he later stated that "Inigo could trace his descent from the best nobility in the province of Guipuscoa." [3] This blood Inigo found impossible to deny even to the day of his death. It was because of this aristocratic family-sense that Inigo, despite all the detachment of his Christian asceticism, could write in later years such submissive letters to the temporal heads of his house, to his brother and to his nephew. This family-sense is, as it were, the prototype of his matured feeling for form, subordination, and obedience.

In addition, a second trait may be pointed out. The Loyolas were provincial nobility, in the best sense of the word. They never lost touch with the peasant world around them. They belonged to the Basque people in the same way the hoary stone blocks of their castle-tower formed part of the mountainous country of Azpeitia. Hence, the little Inigo, the thirteenth and last child, was entrusted soon after his birth to a peasant wet nurse, who was to suckle him with the milk of her breasts during his infancy. We know even her name and the name of her unpretentious farm from the processes for the canonization of Inigo: Maria Garin, from a tiny hamlet called Eguibar, close to the castle of Loyola.[4]

If, as we have said, the Loyola paternal manorial estate partook of a peasant-patriarchal character, then the time of Inigo's early youth was spent partly in the "comparative elegance of the family seat and partly at the modest farm house at Eguibar." [5] Because of this upbringing, Inigo, for the rest of his life, remained a Basque closely linked with the common people. The shrewd peasant proverbs of his keen-sighted fellow countrymen remained embedded in his laconic thinking; and the maxims of the Saint, collected in later years from his writings, give evidence, as a Roman cardinal once testified concerning the aging Saint, of an uncanny knack "for striking the nail on the head." [6]

From the days of his youth utterly discordant elements flowed harmoniously together in the personality of Inigo, as though into a single river bed. In it we find mirrored the dovecotes and white flour dust of the mills and farms of his father's estate, together with the pleasant odor of roasted chestnuts wafted from peasant cottages of Eguibar, the memory of which persisted up to the last years of his life, as he ate his four chestnuts as a special titbit on a feast day. We find mingled together in a curious blend, moreover, the soldier Spanish he picked up from his father and elder soldier brothers and the fine Basque which he learned from his foster mother and in the peasant homes, so much so that this strange mixture cannot be thought of as separate from the crude Spanish which we note in the letters of St. Ignatius during the whole course of his life. We see, too, in the parish church the pew reserved for the nobility that the son of a lord can claim whenever he comes down from the castle to attend mass and vespers; but at the same time we also see the robust, through-and-through Catholic piety of the lord's rural pilgrimages to the hermitages of Olaz and

Elosiaga situated near the castle of Loyola. The courtly
manners of his relative, Juan Anchieta, the archpriest of
the royal chapel at Azpeitia, is closely linked with the ineffaceable impression made upon the youthful Inigo by the
pious folk songs and merry dances of the Basque peasantry,
which Inigo, many years after while a student at Paris,
could re-enact in order to cheer up a fellow companion
suffering from a spiritual affliction. There also we meet
with the mischievous pranks played by Inigo in his ef-
fervescent youth—the thefts of apples, and such deeds—
misdemeanors of which he was later (1535) to accuse himself in the pulpit before all the assembled people. But at
the same time, too, we witness his first trial services in choir
and at the altar—charges which had been entrusted to his
care as a cleric. Finally there is the rod of the pedagogue,
some unhappy cleric of Azpeitia appointed to drive into
the head of the young rascal from the noble castle the
rudiments of writing and arithmetic, which his father with
a grim sense of humor willed to him as his only inheritance.[7]

There is still a third factor to be considered. Inigo was
the last-born child of the family. In the house of Loyola
it was customary for the eldest son to inherit the whole
of the vast and wealthy estate, whereas the other sons
had to shift for themselves and determine how they
could obtain the means of livelihood commensurate with
the standards of their noble rank. Inigo's father, in his
usual patriarchal and arbitrary manner, first considered
securing the future of his youngest son by enrolling him
in the clerical militia. Accordingly his son received the
tonsure while still a mere stripling; his father then engaged a tutor for him at no small expense. But as Inigo
grew to maturity, there also grew in him a stubborn op-

position to this plan of his father's. Nadal, in an as yet inedited manuscript, remarks very aptly concerning the youth of Inigo: "Though he received the education usually given to noblemen's sons, he did not profit any from his studies; soon a sort of noble fire began to burn in his breast, and his thoughts were wholly intent upon the idea of distinguishing himself 'in military glory.' " [8] Inigo was "of Loyola," and that meant a good deal; but he was also "of and at Loyola." The future lay before him, the insecurity of his life had to be removed first; all things were possible for a descendant of Loyola, but first it had to be won! His hands were empty, but in the hopes burgeoning within his youthful breast lay hidden a whole new world. In that consisted the original foundation of his "more."

2. His Education

It was during this carefree period of his youth that Inigo was called upon to make the first decision involving a serious change in his life. When Inigo was fifteen or sixteen (probably in the year 1507), his father, or, in the event of his death, his elder brother, sent him as a page to the princely court of their relative, Don Juan Velasquez de Cuellar, at that time the High Lord Steward, *Contador Major,* of the Catholic Majesties who were residing at Arevalo, from which central point Velasquez followed the royal court in its round of progress. From this time on Inigo forsook the clerical course thrust upon him by his father, though he still clung to the tonsure (thus ready for any possible future contingency).

We should hardly be wrong in maintaining that this step was due to Inigo's own vehement insistence; for he felt that he was fit for something better than the career of country pastor on his father's demesne, where his elder priestly brother had already given a very unsavory example (he left behind him four natural children, to the disgrace of the princely line of Loyola). The pressure of the "more" in Inigo, as yet merely natural and aristocratic, drove him therefore from the service of the Church to the service of an earthly king, since, as a page in the house of Don Juan, he came as a matter of course into contact with the royal court.

It was at this time, too, that he was smitten with an infatuation for a certain lady (and this was, so to speak, the second courtly "more" of the young Loyola). This lady, he tells us many decades later, "was of a higher rank than a mere duchess or countess." [9] She must then have been of the royal lineage—no less, perhaps, than Dona Catarina, the young daughter of Philip the Fair and of the mad Joanna, in whose eerie castle at Tordesillas he was compelled to live for a while as a page of Don Juan de Cuellar.[10]

What Inigo acquired from his contact with these highly aristocratic surroundings was, above all, in addition to the strengthening of his sense of fidelity toward the *Reyes Catolicos,* a sense for what pertained to courtly ritual, a sense for "etiquette" in the best sense of the word. The results of his training at Arevalo are summed up by Fr. Nadal in two words: "He was educated piously and 'nobly.' " [11] The best fruit, however, that he carried away with him from his sojourn at Arevalo was that chivalrous attitude which never left him the rest of his life: to be at last in the service of a king reverenced from afar, to form a part in the mysterious mechanism of "the royal household," even though merely an insignificant page. There was the silent fitting of himself into the royal service, the all-penetrating consciousness of being "at court," the feeling, at first still very unpurified, of being set apart from the common people and of being called to perform deeds that would give him a chance to distinguish himself. In short, there began that attitude which he later transposed to the spiritual realm when he spoke in the meditation on the Kingdom of Christ about "the man who was willing to signalize himself in every kind of service for his King and supreme Lord."

In a different sense, however, Arevalo proved for Inigo a step in his formation for his coming vocation. This period during which Inigo ripened to manhood was a sinful period. The laconic allusions of the *Autobiography* of the Saint were filled out by Polanco in the following way: "Though he always remained faithfully attached to his religion, still he did not always live according to its prescriptions and was not always on guard against sin; he especially indulged in gambling, duelling, and romances with women." [12] He persevered in this line of conduct even after his return home to Loyola, where, in 1515—hence in his twenty-fourth year—he was even cited before court for some mysterious affair. Exclude this experience of his sinful youth and it will be impossible to comprehend his knack for the discernment of spirits, manifesting itself so powerfully on his sickbed at Loyola; indeed this discernment of spirits is nothing

more than an intensified continuance of the inner tur-
moil that had been going on for years, of the civil war
raging between his knightly sense of honor and the
shameful yielding to "dark" inclinations. He who characterized himself a man "who experienced within himself a powerful but vain longing for fame" [13] was at the
same time a man "who succumbed to the vices of the
flesh." [14] This is a typical experience which we find described for all times in the pages of St. Augustine's *Confessions.* In the case of St. Ignatius, it is rendered acute
by his chivalrous sense of violated decency, the typically
Ignatian "shame," upon which he later laid so much stress
in his Spiritual Exercises and which he symbolized (First
Week, Second Annotation) by the image "of the recreant
knight, standing full of shame and confusion before his
king and the whole royal court." (This image of the
knight serves at the same time as the introduction to the
Second Week and its chivalrous attitude in the meditation on the Kingdom of Christ.) On the other hand, it is
to be noted that Ignatius never at any time, neither here
nor elsewhere, permitted himself the luxury of a too
frank confession of his past sinful life or of painful self-
recriminations. Such things, he held, were things to be
settled in private between God and the soul and were to
be got rid of in almost scrupulously exact general
confessions. Even during the mystic peace of his latter
years (for example, before his election to the generalate
in 1541), such matters were to be humbly hidden in the
bosom of "the hierarchical Church" in sacramental general reviews. Before men, the chivalrous attitude demanded that a deep veil of silence be spread over the sins

he had committed in the past, no less than over the mystic graces which he had received. Reserve and shame go together. The most sublime and the most abysmal things of his life are matters to be dealt with before His Royal Majesty alone. This chivalrous attitude, the fruit of his training and education, was the real seed of his "discreet love."

3. Conclusions

From the formation outlined so far springing from his descent and education, a few further deductions can be drawn which relate the ideal of perfection presented in the book of the Spiritual Exercises to the ideal exemplified in the Company of Jesus. Let us first touch on the ideal of perfection held out by the Exercises. A mere glance at the contents makes it evident that in a man such as Inigo the illuminating grace of Manresa had to be connected with his earthly ideals of a king. Behind these ideals which had hitherto swayed Inigo—behind his inborn loyalty to the *Reyes Catolicos* and their religio-political ideals world-wide in extent; behind the roving phantasies of gallant knights galloping far and wide in search of daring feats to perform (feats that would bring them distinction in the eyes of their royal master, feats that his imagination painted so vividly and of which he was so fond of reading in his precious romances of love); behind his romantic love for a lady of high degree; behind the ideal of iron discipline in the military service which he chose as his calling (a discipline casually submitted to, yet which demanded standing in alert readiness at an assigned post, a military service assuming, after the merry days of Arevalo and the tragic fall of his first master in 1517, the character of frighteningly serious war duties under the leadership of the Duke of Najera) —behind all these ideals, I say, there rose up a new ideal beckoning him, an ideal so sharp and vivid in outline as to be able almost to be grasped with the hands, an ideal just as noble but wholly different in nature: the ideal of service under an eternal king. We can see an instance of this transposition in the working out of the exercise on the Kingdom of Christ. God is called "His Divine Majesty," up to and including the contemplation for gaining Divine Love (*Spiritual Exercises,* nn. 98, 146, 147, 233).[14a] The Blessed Trinity is "seated on the royal dais or throne of His Divine Majesty" (no. 106) even at the moment of the marvelous condescension in the Incarnation; and around His Majesty is His "heavenly court" (the *corte* or *corte celestial*); God is "His Majesty" not merely when the sinful knight stands in deepest shame before the king and his court, but even at that supreme moment, when at the highest pitch of enthusiasm, the knight makes a fresh oblation of himself to the Divine Majesty—nay, even at the time when in the highest flight of love he unites himself with God in the most intimate communion (no. 232). The only reply worthy of a man animated by the sentiments of a true nobleman to the appeal of the Divine King is the "more" of the offering of himself to perform deeds of distinction: a *senalarse mas en servicio,* that is, a signalizing of himself in service, an offering of *oblaciones de mayor stima,* that is, offerings of greater value; or, as the first Latin

version has it, an *oblatio praecisior,* "an ever more
sharply defined offering." * In his estimation, anything
of less value or more in conformity with hard common
sense, would be unworthy of His Divine Majesty. But
since such a tawdry offering is out of the question in the
mind of a true knight, and since he does not make a
great ado of his clear, calm surrender, it follows that his
"more" immediately becomes an offering of "homage
and obedience" (no. 92), a "service of the Eternal
Father" (no. 135), just as it was in the case of Christ
Himself. The Ignatian ideal of the Spiritual Exercises,
therefore, is contained in the four words: *senalarse mas
en servicio,* "to distinguish oneself more in His service."

What we have just said about the ideal of perfection
of the Spiritual Exercises holds true equally for the ideal
of perfection of the Society which grew out of them. By
his very lineage Ignatius was fitted to found a "Company," to plan and bring into existence an Order that
would be the embodiment of the words *senalarse mas en
servicio,* "to distinguish oneself more in the service of
God." The foundation for two of the more characteristic
qualities of his Society, obedience and discipline, seems
to have been laid in the natural preparation of Ignatius
for the lifework marked out for him by God.

First, obedience. Considered from the viewpoint described above, it is already plain just why this disposition
of obedience had to play such an essential role in the
Order he founded. Like Inigo at Arevalo, every Jesuit is

* Actually the Latin version has *oblatio praeciosior,* "a more
precious offering," which Father Rahner seems to have mis-
read.—Translator's note.

a member of a royal household, is ever ready for service in the household of his king, who is constantly changing his place of residence; and is ever alert at his assigned post and has no leisure to become attached through monastic contemplation and exclusive spiritual self-sanctification to a fixed dress, set manner of fighting, or permanent habitat. For him obedience means alertness, kept ever bright and shining by fresh exercise, to the divine call—a call conveyed to him by a gradation of human means; a Jesuit's obedience is characterized by a readiness to accept the wholly unexpected, never to build for himself a "comfortable nest," and never to be a soldier unarmed. Obedience is nothing else than the "more" of service carried out in the activity of daily life.[15]

Secondly, in regard to discipline. This is simply the religious form of that "attitude" in the ideal of Ignatius which resulted from his training as a nobleman. It is the opposite of what is impulsive, the sworn enemy of sensuality in every form, even the most refined. Discipline connotes shame, reserve, aristocratic reticence, instinctive shrinking from too great familiarity with any particular person, love of plan even to regimentation, flight from all that refuses to submit to control and regulation. It is fond of the conventional and conservative, even the "old-fashioned." Discipline shuns all forms of ostentation, posing, putting on airs, especially and precisely in that which is the highest of all things—in the service of God. In a word, discipline is bodily and spiritual purity.

This characteristic St. Ignatius impressed most deeply on the ideal of his Order. Hence life in the Society of

Jesus is not a "cozy" life, nor have its houses that celestial-terrestrial atmosphere of deep-rooted stability found in the monasteries of St. Benedict, or that romantic *poverello* air displayed by Capuchin convents. This trait accounts for that feeling of aloofness which prevails among fellow Jesuits, leading them to address one another in a more polite and formal manner, and inducing them to govern their dealings with the outside world by "the rules of modesty" worked out by the "Senor of Loyola." It may be that by adopting this way of acting the Jesuit loses contact with the outside ordinary world, a contact so often and so unnecessarily praised. Such a line of conduct may even be an advantage to him, provided he does not turn this feeling of reserve into a systematic habit, but cultivates the attitude solely because it is a "representation" of the fact that the Kingdom of God "suffereth violence," that His Divine Majesty is to be approached only with awed reverence, and that the mysteries of our holy Faith do not admit of any and every sort of familiarity. The Jesuit ideal stands for "disciplined service," which is, however, "the boundless love of the 'more' confined within the limits of the discretion of obedience." The distinctive mark of this attitude's authenticity is the "noble" discipline, that cleanness of the interior life and its outward relations, which is in accord with one of the wisest maxims bequeathed to us by Ignatius: "Do not mingle indiscriminately with the multitude; shun particular friendships. Take counsel with your spirit and see whither it is leading and driving you. Note carefully in what direction the motions of the spirit are seeking to lead you." [16] This procedure was observed by Ignatius even down to the most minute external details of everyday life. Basically his almost fastidious feeling for physical cleanliness [17] sprang from the same disposition as his instinctive distrust of the extravagant manifestations in mystics.[18] The form his love of poverty took always remained "noble." Father Benedetto Palmio, the minister of the professed house at Rome, has given us a description of what was customary in the refectory during the regime of Ignatius: "The appointments at table, to be sure, always breathed a love of simplicity and poverty, but over all there hung an indefinable air of court etiquette (*nescio quid aulicum tamen redolebat*). As a rule, two or three were appointed to serve at table, especially when distinguished visitors had been invited. At such a time the wine-glasses were 'credenced' with a decorum and elegance, such as could not have been surpassed in any princely court." [19] For the Jesuit, discipline is the discretion of the "more" carried into daily life.

Thus the noble stock from which he sprang and the training and education which he received already lay bare before our eyes the skeleton outlines of his future ideal. The Spiritual Exercises and the Society of Jesus reveal themselves "as it were, from below," as the work of a nobleman and of a soldier. Their ideal is the "more" of a chivalrous disposition, but one which developed into the discretion of service.

Chapter 2

The Impact of the Tradition of Christian Piety Upon Ignatius

THERE is no ideal of perfection in the Church that did not have to prove its genuineness by the manner in which it fitted into the framework of the visible Mystical Body of Christ. Hence every Christian ideal of perfection represents an historical fact of tradition, because the Church of its very nature is something that has been handed down by the Apostles through the Fathers. In the history of the Church, every form of asceticism and mysticism that tried in pure intellectual pride to break away from humble dependence on the heritage of the past; or that sought to overleap the centuries in order to see in a former, primitive Church its ideal and pretended that all further growth and development was simply an excess and departure from the true path, has ended up in subjectivism and sterility. This is the profound thought expressed in the preface to the Ignatian Constitutions, where, among other scales of measurement, we find the "spirit of love" also measured by the examples of the

16

saints. Ignatius sets down there merely what he personally experienced from the first moment of his conversion. His ideal of perfection is also enkindled by the example of saints and consequently follows a pattern that can be accurately indicated from historical sources. "But in that castle none of the books he habitually and so passionately read were to be found; so they gave him *The Life of Christ* and *The Lives of the Saints,* both in Spanish." [20] In these words Ignatius describes the exact point at which the stream of traditional Christian perfection began to enter his soul. But the reason this contact acted so powerfully toward bringing about a new life in Ignatius was that, in some way or other, he had already been prepared for it. Consequently, we must now consider two things: first, the remote preparation of his soul for the appeal of the traditional voices of Christian perfection; and secondly, the actual process of this contact and its essential consequences in the forming of his ideal.

1. Ignatius' Preparation

The primitive form in which contact with Christian tradition is usually established within the soul is the religious training in the parental home. Inigo was not a mere "untutored barbarian" in matters of piety. He has been described as such at various times and by various authors in order to make the startling character of his sudden conversion stand out in sharper contrast. [21] He had not only a noble but also a pious education. Both he and his most intimate fellow Jesuits always deemed it worthwhile to insist that he had constantly remained

faithful to his religion from youth, with an irreproach-
able, never-doubting fidelity. "In my country we have
no Jews," was the retort of Ignatius to the ecclesiastical
inquisitor at Alcala.[22] That was a pregnant phrase in the
Spain of those days. Nadal penned the following words
in regard to him in after years: "Ignatius is a Spaniard,
an offspring of the best nobility of Guipuzcoa, of a
family in which stainless faith has ever been preserved
intact. The zeal for, and constancy in, their religion
among the inhabitants was so great, and their adherence
to their faith so stubborn, that they would not suffer any
converts to live with them; nay, from immemorial times,
from the days when Christianity was first planted in that
land, no one has ever been found who had incurred even
the suspicion of heresy." [23]

This primitively Christian environment of his native
land was introduced into the Loyolan household by Mag-
dalena de Araoz, the wife of Inigo's eldest brother, when
she became chatelaine of Loyola castle. She had brought
with her as a part of her dowry the beautiful picture of
the Annunciation still extant in the domestic chapel of
Loyola, before which Inigo often prayed; she brought
also the four large de luxe volumes of *The Life of Christ*
which had just then appeared in Spanish and which
would soon play such an important role in Inigo's conversion. Her advent evidently brought into the whole
household a spirit of Spanish-Castilian refinement and
culture, of fresh devotion. From that period of his early
life, Inigo kept an eye for religious works of art; and, at
the very eve of his setting out for Manresa, we behold
him still expending the last ducats of his pay from the

Duke of Najera "to have a picture of our blessed Lady which was in poor condition restored as beautifully as possible." [24] At any rate, some fleeting memories of spiritual things may still have survived from the days when, with the aid of a pedagogue, his father had made his sad attempts to enroll him into the clerical militia. In Arevalo, however, at the court of Don Juan de Cuellar, Inigo stepped into a spiritual world that left unmistakable traces in the life of his soul.

At that time, owing to the piety of Don Juan and of two ladies, his wife and mother-in-law, both of whom rivalled him in devotion, Arevalo was the focal center of the new Franciscan spirit of reform—a reform which the genius-like figure of Cardinal de Cisneros had taken under his wing. Here, and afterwards in the palace of the Duke of Najera at Navarette, Inigo came into contact for the first time with a tradition of spiritual life which had made itself vividly felt. In the convent of the Poor Clares at Arevalo, founded by Don Juan de Cuellar, hymns were sung which had been composed by the Franciscan, Fray Ambrosio de Montesino, in honor of St. Francis of Assisi and dedicated to Dona Maria de Guevara, the Basque mother-in-law of Don Juan and friend of the youthful Inigo. Undoubtedly, Inigo was familiar with the verses which celebrate in song (and in a typically Spanish fashion) the *poverello* as the brave *caudillo*, laying siege to the three menacing fortresses of the world, the flesh, and the devil.[25] His later interest in the heroic figure of St. Francis is bound up with such recollections. Fray Ambrosio (who also translated into Spanish Ludolph of Saxony's *The Life of Christ* and so

made it possible for the wounded Loyola to read this
work) dedicated still another book of verses, entitled
The Way of the Cross, to the Duchess of Najera. Again
there can be no doubt that Inigo read these poems at
Navarrete. There is not the least doubt that in these
years so fruitful for his spiritual life, Inigo read the epic
of another poet, *Triumphs of the Apostles* by Juan de
Padilla. At that time Inigo, strange to say, even tried his
hand at writing verses himself! "It would be curious to
see," observes Astrain, not without a tinge of irony,
"what the poetry of this man would be like since he had
so much difficulty in writing prose all his life long." [26]
Inigo wrote an epic at that time on St. Peter, the Prince
of the apostles,[27] for whom, as he himself confesses, "he
had a very special devotion." [28] It is no wonder that the
Saint of the hastily drawn sword, the patron of the
Basque hermitage at Eguimendiga near Loyola castle,
the patron likewise of the fortress church at Arevalo,
where the page had to spend so much time at divine
services, must have had a special appeal for him. Undoubtedly, the fine songs of Juan de Padilla composed in
honor of St. Peter furnished him a model for his own
poems. The *Triumphs of the Apostles* by this poet occa-
sionally gives a glowing description of the beauties a
pious soul can find in the Carthusian monastery of Santa
Maria de las Cuevas at Seville; as a consequence, several
years afterwards, while tied to his bed at Loyola, Inigo
conceived a lively desire to enter this far-distant monastery, and not the Carthusian monastery of Miraflores at
Burgos, as some have falsely imagined, though the latter
would certainly have been nearer for a Basque.[29] From

all of this we can conclude that Inigo did read the poems of de Padilla. Consequently, there was, on the one hand, a possibility of effecting a connection between these and many other religious impressions, even though these were vague and half-understood, and, on the other, the future struggle between the good and bad spirits in the soul of Inigo. How strange a mixture the religious milieu at Arevalo and Navarette and his still unpurified worldly spirit had formed in the heart of Inigo, we learn from an observation of his cousin, Father Araoz, who knew him well. He says, "Just before engaging in a duel, he used to compose verses in honor of our Lady." [30] Here we have the same old Inigo who even after his conversion, in order to vindicate the insulted honor of our Blessed Lady, wished to stab the offending Moor with his dagger.[31]

As yet "he was blind, yet full of desire to serve God as he best knew how"; [32] or, as Polanco puts it, "Up to his conversion, very little of his time was devoted to the exercise of spiritual things." [33] But what is characteristic of his whole knightly attitude we gather from the sources wherein Ignatius and others testify to the spiritual state of his soul during this period of knightly preparation. These particulars tell us that he never blasphemed,[34] for to some degree he felt within himself a sense of reverence for the Divine Majesty; that he had an instinctive aversion for every form of lying and that "he was very conscientious regarding this point even then";[35] that he had a fully developed, aristocratic feeling for spiritual purity; that he was entirely free from all attachment to money and earthly possessions. In his eyes, as Polanco aptly remarks, such an attachment would have been considered

dishonorable.[36] Hence, shortly after he had been wounded
at Pampeluna, he gave his shield, armor, and dagger to
those who had transported him to the castle of Loyola.

With a man of this caliber God could begin great undertakings for His glory. As Polanco testifies, the distinctive trait of Inigo's whole nature and of his piety, too,
even in the dark days of sin and worldly life, was a magnanimous disposition of soul, a deeply planted urge to
carry out difficult things, combined with an unerring
prudence.[37] Again, this manner of showing his piety, the
net result of the traditions in his parental home and of
his aristocratic upbringing, formed an immediate preparation for the "more" of his service in the battleline of
his eternal King, into the ranks of whose army he is now
deployed as a consequence of his conversion.

2. His Conversion

We shall not fix our attention, here, upon the process
of his conversion in its totality, but only upon its suitabil-
ity for a deeper historical understanding of the ideal of
the Spiritual Exercises, now coming to light for the first
time in the movements of his soul as a result of his conversion. But here, too, we are face to face (without being
under the necessity of reshuffling historical facts in order
to prove a mere theory or to make a convenient division)
with the two chief components which at once unite with
life-giving force, like an embryonic plasma. They are the
matter and form, as it were, of the coming Spiritual Exercises: namely, chivalrous service of Christ the eternal
King in warfare against Satan, together with the urging

of the "more" toward distinguishing oneself in that service; and prudence, cooly weighing the pros and cons, scenting out all possibilities, discerning spirits. We have again, therefore, the Ignatian ideal of "discreet" love; and, thanks to the prudent notes (prudent to the point of genius) which St. Ignatius himself dictated, we are able to reconstruct the very earliest beginnings of this ideal.

It is a well-known fact that the Spiritual Exercises have been subjected to research from every possible angle for the purpose of discovering real or pretended sources from which Inigo de Loyola is supposed to have drawn his teaching. Inigo, no doubt, would have had nothing but a smile of kindly pity or, we may suppose, of gentle irony, had it been his lot to behold the historizing vivisection that his little work, which caused him such immense painstaking, would undergo in later times. It is right to assert, as some have done, that if Inigo had consulted all the sources that, in all academic seriousness, he has been "proved" to have consulted, he must have had, at the time of his sojourn in the cave of Manresa, a stately library of Latin and Spanish authors. It has been supposed by others that the chief source for the Ignatian streams of piety was to be found in the "modern devotion" (*devotio moderna*) of the fifteenth century. Successively, Cisneros, Erasmus of Rotterdam, Alonzo de Madrid, Gerard of Zütphen, John Maubernus, even Werner of Saint Blaise and Pseudo-Bernard, who flourished at the height of the Middle Ages, were rated as "indubitably" proven authorities for whole sections in the text of the Exercises. This course has led nowhere.

What, in the end, was the upshot of all these laborious inquiries? Nothing but the simple fact that Inigo read only these three books: *The Life of Christ* of Ludolph of Saxony, *The Golden Legend,* and *The Imitation of Christ.* Furthermore, we can show many traces of these three works in the Spiritual Exercises—the statements, for example, that Adam was created in the regions around Damascus, that Joseph and Mary on their journey to Bethlehem had an ass and a servant-maid, that Mary's parents divided their property into three parts, and other trifling minutiae which are to be found in Ludolph of Saxony. But of what earthly use is all this quibbling for giving us a deeper comprehension of the genesis and development of the Spiritual Exercises? St. Ignatius himself, in his "pilgrimage" journal, testifies in the clearest manner to the fact that he read three books only. To establish that fact there is no need of elaborate investigations. We even know the editions of the works he made use of. *The Life of Christ* by the German Carthusian, Ludolph of Saxony, was that which had been translated into Spanish by Fray Ambrosio Montesino and published at Alcala in 1502–03. He read *The Golden Legend* by Jacopo de Voragine in the Spanish translation by the Cistercian Goberto Maria Vagad, which appeared at Saragossa in 1493 and was reprinted at Toledo in 1511. Concerning *The Imitation of Christ,* St. Ignatius himself confesses: "It was at Manresa that I saw the *Gerçonzito* for the first time, and since then there is no other book of devotion that I like more." [38] The *Gerçonzito* is one of the innumerable Spanish editions of *The Imitation of Christ.* It was called the *Gerçonzito* because it was generally ascribed at that time to Gerson, the one-time chancellor of the University of Paris.

The question before us now may be reduced to this: Is it possible to show where the contact-point, so to speak, between the tradition of Christian perfection and Inigo's own disposition for greatness arose in his heart as he whiled away the tedium of his long convalescence by reading these books, and is it possible to show it in such a way that the cell-forms begin to manifest signs of growth and development?

Two observations of Ignatius facilitate the answer to this fundamental question. His first remark tells us that he made excerpts from *The Life of Christ* with incredible diligence, entering with his own hand the "more important matters," after going over them prayerfully, into a notebook of three hundred densely crowded quarto pages.[39] His second remark preserves for us two memories of his first spiritual readings, recollections that left a lifelong impression on him. In his "pilgrimage" journal, he narrates how his mind was continually haunted by the thought: "What would happen if I acted as St. Francis and St. Dominic did?"[40] And on one occasion he told Nadal, "At that period of my life I was filled with desire to do great things in the service of God, such as had been done by St. Onuphrius and other saints who gave themselves unreservedly to Him."[41]

To do great things—this is the first foundation of the Exercises, the seedling form of the "more." As yet Inigo is wholly ignorant of spiritual matters and the various fluctuating spirits which possess his soul, tossing him from "the great things" to be done for worldly, military

fame and for love of his Dona to "the greater things" to
be done for God. "He always set himself hard and difficult tasks to perform," [42] he says when speaking of this
life-generating chaos which he experienced within himself. Now his reading opened to him an entirely new
world, a world in which his pent up forces could break
forth in a manner wholly different from that which had
been possible under the sway of his former ideals, now
so strangely insipid.

The first pages of these two books, which he kept by
his bedside, set the whole conflict in motion. Precisely
here we have the first approaches toward the substance
of the ideal of the Spiritual Exercises: the Kingdom of
Christ and the noble following of that king in chivalrous
service.

Fray Ambrosio Montesino begins by dedicating his
work, *The Life of Christ,* to their Catholic Majesties,
Ferdinand and Isabella:

May it please the sacred majesty of your Royal High-
nesses never to forget that the dominion of earthly kings is
nothing else than (to use the phrase of St. John Chrysos-
tom) a symbol and figure of the everlasting and unchang-
ing kingdom which good kings will enjoy in heaven after
all earthly dominion, which flits by like a shadow, will
have passed away. . . . But it is a sign and seal of future
kingly and immortal dominion, when earthly kings show
themselves more concerned with what pertains to the royal
dominion of God and even make use of calamities and
scourges, which a mysterious Providence of God sends, in
order to advance in reverence and service of their eternal
and sovereign King.[43]

These words were read by Inigo in those tedious days, read with a disposition of soul which he himself has so aptly described in the following words, "with a magnanimous heart, inflamed by God." [44] The preface affixed to *The Golden Legend* by the Cistercian Goberto Vagad showed him the way such greater service for his King could be performed. On the title page of *The Life of Christ* there was a portrait of their Catholic Majesties, whom Inigo had served with enthusiasm. On the title page of *The Golden Legend* we find a life-sized picture of the crucified Saviour. To this Fray Goberto appended the following remarks:

It is understood that we should fix our gaze upon the sublime power, the incomparable, incomprehensible, more than kingly magnanimity shining forth from the Passion and death of the King of Kings and Lord of Lords, who is a portal, so to speak, through which we enter into the saintly and glorious life of the blessed. Whoever reads this book should grasp the crucifix with his right hand and hold it aloft as a royal standard bringing with it victory and happiness, as an incentive spurring generous souls to an eternal triumph, as an emblem which armed the chivalrous hearts of the saints for a courageous conquest of the world, the flesh, and the devil, who, together with all his infernal satellites, far outstrips all the damned in astuteness and adroitness.[45]

Can anyone fail to see how this natural as well as acquired "noble" magnanimity of Inigo links up with the ideal that is the innermost core of the Spiritual Exercises? Yet this connection will be made even plainer by another extract that Inigo culled from the life of St.

Augustine in *The Golden Legend*. There we read that
St. Augustine's object in writing his classic opus, *The
City of God,* was to portray the historic battle for the
salvation of the world between Christ and Satan; "that
his book was concerned with the story of two cities, with
the kings of these two cities, Jerusalem and Babylon. For
Christ is king over Jerusalem, Satan over Babylon. Two
contrary loves gave birth to these cities. The city of Satan
was built on self-love, mounting up even to contempt of
God; the city of Christ was built on love of God, mounting up even to the contempt of self." [46]

In view of the excerpts just cited, what need is there
to waste time exploring every imaginable avenue of research; what need to establish, for instance, that for his
meditation on the Two Standards (a basic meditation in
the whole structure of the Spiritual Exercises) Ignatius'
authority was Pseudo-Bernard or Werner of St. Blaise or
some other ascetical writer? No, his whole method of
procedure was much simpler. Inigo's soul underwent
long preparation in prayerful reading of these texts from
The Golden Legend before the basic law of the Kingdom of Christ flashed upon him. (He informs us that he
spent his time partly in prayer, partly in copying out excerpts.) [47] *The Golden Legend,* written in Latin by a
pious Dominican in the thirteenth century and translated
into Spanish by a holy Franciscan in the fifteenth century, gave Inigo an immediate contact with the Christian
tradition classically formulated by Augustine's theology
of history. [48] This classic narrative was clothed in a style
so graphically simple but of such vivid power that it
made an ineffaceable impression upon Inigo, who was as

yet untrained in the ways of spiritual thinking but who
was deeply agitated and perplexed by the mysterious
motions of the different spirits within him. "Thus it
came about gradually," he dictated in later years, "that
he began to recognize the difference between the spirits
that agitated him, the spirit of God and the spirit of
Satan, and this was the very first meditation he ever
made in regard to spiritual things. When later on he had
made the Exercises himself, he began to draw light from
this former experience for his teaching on the discernment of spirits." [49]

We must therefore firmly hold to the view that these
first spiritual experiences were produced in him, not
solely and exclusively by scrutiny of the interior movements in his soul, but also, and accompanying it, by the
reading of these two, so to say, "conversion" works. Consequently, even at this early date, the notion of the war-
ring Kingdom of Christ had already begun to dawn
upon him; the powerful divine light which bathed his
soul at Manresa would bring to definitive completion
the form of the meditation on the Kingdom of Christ as
we now see it in the Spiritual Exercises.

But the formal element of this ideal of the Spiritual
Exercises that was beginning to develop—the pressure of
the "more" of a generous love which counted no cost
and was filled with enthusiasm for the kingly ideal—also
took fire from the reading of these so-called conversion
books. The ever-fresh power of the words of the New
Testament (in *The Life of Christ*), copied by Inigo in
red ink, lifted him into regions of the spirit hitherto unknown to him; this "more," as yet little understood, he

immediately translated "into the difficult undertaking"
of a pilgrimage to Jerusalem, to the very places where
the Saviour's whole life was spent and where the cross
stood, "the banner and insignia of the whole world's
salvation," to use a phrase often employed by Ludolph
of Saxony.[50] The idea of a pilgrimage, as Inigo himself
reveals, "soon absorbed all his thought," and took even
stronger possession of his soul than the longing for the
Carthusian monastery in Seville. For, in his own words,
"He feared he would not be as free in a Carthusian
convent to put into practice the hatred he had conceived
against himself as he would be on a pilgrimage through
the whole world." [51] In this we hear an echo of Augustine's famous dictum, "the love of God growing more
and more even to hatred of self" (*crescens usque ad
contemptum sui*). Here we watch the great soul of Inigo
as it begins to swell under the uneasy crescendo of the
"more" to which Manresa and its awesome penances are
shortly to bear witness.

In addition to this compelling principle of love and
his assimilation to Christ's annihilation on the cross, in
some way or other anticipated even in the midst of his
strange penitential orgies, another motive now comes
into play—namely, the example of the saints, "the
knights of the cross," [52] principally those saints who had
a special attraction for him: Onuphrius, Francis, and
Dominic. After the lapse of more than thirty years, Ignatius could still recall the profound impression made
upon him by the life and unheard-of penitential works of
Onuphrius, the ancient desert monk from the Egyptian
Thebaid. Like him, Inigo now became enthusiastic about

a rough garment of sackcloth and "an exclusive diet of
herbs." [53] The "Life of Onuphrius," in *The Golden
Legend,* assigns the deeper motive for these practices; by
them the battle with "the enemy of the human race" (a
phrase that Inigo continued to use for the rest of his
life) is fought to the finish. These are "the great things
in the service of God" which Inigo, according to his own
testimony, sought to imitate in the life of Onuphrius; for
while reading he felt the same interior urging to higher
things which Onuphrius expressed to his visitor Paphnutius in those beautiful, legend-like words: "Ever bear in
mind, as I do, what joy and glory those will enjoy in
heaven who have fought the good fight here on earth.
My heart burns within me and my spirit bounds with joy
at the prospect of giving up all earthly pleasures and of
surrendering myself up to God with the whole energy of
my soul." [54] For the meditating Inigo, Onuphrius has
become the model of the man who has "a generous heart
inflamed by the love of God."

The genesis of the Ignatian ideal stands out even more
clearly, perhaps, when we consider the example of the
two other saints, Dominic and Francis, whom St. Ignatius still mentioned by name in 1553, when he was
dictating the reminiscences of his life. St. Francis was
already long familiar to Inigo through the pious poetic
circle at Arevalo, where he had been celebrated in song
"as the valiant captain of the soldiers fighting against the
three fortresses of the world, the flesh, and the devil." [55]
Now (that is, during his convalescence) Inigo had the
opportunity of reading in *The Golden Legend* the de-

lightful story in which Francis and Dominic are brought together:

One night, during his sojourn in Rome to obtain the confirmation of his Order, St. Dominic beheld a vision: He saw Christ hovering above a cloud and holding in His hands three spears which He was about to hurl at the earth. Kneeling at His feet was His Blessed Mother, who asked Him what He was about to do. Jesus answered her, "The whole world is filled with three vices: pride, avarice, and sensual pleasure. I have therefore resolved to destroy it with these three lances." His mother replied, "Have pity, my dear Son, and let Your just indignation be turned into mildness." Our Blessed Lord responded, "Do you not see how they insult Me?" She answered in turn, "My Child, restrain Your wrath and be patient for the moment, for I know of a true servant and a brave knight who is traveling up and down the whole world in order to subjugate it to Your royal dominion. I associate him with another true servant, as a companion in arms, vying with him in fiery zeal and courage." Jesus responded, "Your plea has pacified Me, but I am now anxious to behold these two men regarding whom you have made such great promises." Then Mary presented St. Dominic. Christ said, "Truly, this man is a good and brave knight." After this Mary introduced St. Francis, and Christ bestowed equal praise upon him.[56]

To compete as a good knight "in fervor and courage" with Dominic and Francis was the spiritual experience of Inigo on his sickbed at Loyola. Here his "more" was enkindled; here his longing "to accomplish great and difficult things for Christ" was born. Inigo must have felt that the words at the very beginning of the life of St. Francis in *The Golden Legend* were meant for him:

"Francis was a merchant and up to his twentieth year led a worldly and dissipated life. Then God pricked him with the goad of sickness, and overnight he was changed into a wholly different man. . . . He heard a voice speaking to him, 'Francis, if you really wish to know Me, seek sweetness in bitter things and despise thyself.' " [57] In this case, too, Augustine's self-contempt has the final word, a self-contempt that leads first to God, then to the surprising experience that in the kingdom of the spirit bitter things may become sweet, and sweet things insipid, and lastly to the discernment of spirits, already commencing to work at the base of his enthusiasm. There was yet lacking in the spiritual thinking of Ignatius that depth which will be imparted to him at Manresa "from above," as it were, by mystical grace. All he could think of at this time was to repeat over and over again: "St. Dominic did this, therefore I also must do it; St. Francis did this, therefore I too will do it." [58] But "from the sides"—that is, by the tradition of Christian perfection—Inigo has already been molded. (One might almost be tempted to say "finally molded.") He too has the ambition to become a knight of Christ, wandering over the whole globe in the interests of the Kingdom of his Lord, in order to overcome Satan; and to do this by means of severe penances after the example of his crucified King of Kings, urged on by the passion to signalize himself by the "noble" willingness to serve, now turned into the Christian willingness to serve.

At this point the ideal of Christian perfection looming before the gaze of the convalescing Inigo enters into the

stream of historical tradition, beating upon the soul of
Inigo with its last dying waves. That tradition consisted
in the heroic renunciation of the world made by Egyptian
monasticism in its exaggerated effort at union with God,
in the best fruits of Augustinian theology and spirituality,
in the high medieval spirit of Franciscan-Dominican reform, and in German mysticism's tender love of Jesus.
But this "influence" of tradition took on the form of the
vessel into which it was poured. We must never forget
that it is the noble grandee and the soldier who permits
himself to suffer this "influence" of tradition, and that
consequently whatever he reads in these two cherished
sick-room books resolves itself into a deeper perception
of those two truths which form the innermost core of the
future Spiritual Exercises: the Kingdom of Christ and
the Two Standards. There can be no doubt that he
possessed this insight at the moment of his departure for
the pilgrimage to Montserrat and Manresa. In one of his
exhortations, Father Olivares, a very close friend of
Ignatius in his old age, says as much. "From the very
outset of his conversion, even while on the road to Montserrat and to a secluded spot near Manresa, his mind
was totally preoccupied with two meditations: the Two
Standards and his King setting out to wage war on
Satan and the whole world." [59] It remained necessary
only for the mystical grace of Manresa to purify this insight. The knight of Christ (whom the Blessed Virgin
commends to her royal Son, as in the legend of Dominic)
now consecrates his sword to Our Lady of Montserrat
and imagines that he ought to begin the brave fight at

once by stabbing several times a Moor who had insulted the Blessed Virgin. The illumination which was to change him completely was still lacking.

Thus he wended his way to Montserrat, his mind constantly fixed on the great feats he longed to perform for the love of God in the service of his royal Master. And since his mind was entirely taken up with the tales he had read in his beloved romances of love and books of a similar nature, he resolved to keep a vigil of arms for a whole night before the altar of Our Lady of Montserrat and to doff his usual princely garments and put on the livery of Christ.[60]

It was only through the mystical grace of Manresa that he was to grasp fully in what the "livery of Christ" really consisted, namely, in the ignominy of Christ that leads to the glory of the Father. It was at Manresa, too, that all his previous spiritual experiences were reduced to those skeleton notes which form the backbone, so to speak, of the Exercises: the Kingdom of Christ and the battle between the two camps, the outcome of which battle, both in general history and in individuals, hangs upon the saying "Yes" to the shame of the cross. Accordingly, in his dialogues on the Institute, Father Nadal remarks, "Here at Manresa God communicated to Inigo the Spiritual Exercises and by this means led him to give himself wholly to the service of the glory of God and the salvation of souls. That God wished him to do so he learned chiefly from two meditations, the Kingdom of Christ and the Two Standards." [61]

3. Conclusions

From this embryonic form of the Loyolan ideal, as described above, it is possible to make some deductions that lead us to a deeper understanding of the Spiritual Exercises and the Society of Jesus.

First, in regard to the Spiritual Exercises. We now perceive more clearly that the meditations on the Kingdom and the Two Standards constitute the real heart of the Exercises, are its "principle and foundation"; however, we are not to confuse them with the Principle and Foundation, the opening consideration. For although the Exercises must start with the Principle and Foundation of the First Week, it is the call of the King and the spectacular array of the two camps that form the real foundation for an economy of salvation. Everything in the Exercises which precedes and follows these two key meditations takes its significance from them; all that precedes, because only after them do we see with such clarity what Ignatius intended in his Principle and Foundation which be prefixed to his First Week. Only after these Exercises does their theology become apparent, progressing as it does from creation, through indifference, to that which "conduces more to the end for which we were created." But why and for what end we were created we can learn only from Christ our Lord; we can learn in what the "more" consists, since now it receives a more significant development, though in itself it appears illogical and meaningless. All this provides a new solution to the question whether or not the Foundation is primarily and solely concerned with natural creation and the consequences which flow from it, and whether it is therefore merely a preparatory theodicy. This is not the case at all. It is, then, incumbent upon us to imbue the meditation on the Foundation with the Christological spirit, without in any way sacrificing its introductory character of laying bare the mere outlines and nerves, so to speak, of the Spiritual Exercises. We must try therefore to make the meditation assume the striking shape in which it occured to Inigo on his sickbed as he looked on the title page of *The Golden Legend* and, "lifting his gaze to the starry heavens, felt himself moved by a strong desire to serve God, our Lord," [62] and consequently to serve also Christ crucified, Creator of heaven, earth, and himself.

The same Christological influence applies also to the First Week. Its meaning, in the first place, does not consist in a purification from sin for the sake of making a good general confession (though it has that meaning also), but its whole motivating force is derived from the contemplation on the Kingdom of Christ and the Two Standards. It is Christological even to the point where the cross stands at the brink of hell, where all sinners of all time are divided according to the position they have taken toward the Incarnate Word, where the question is wrung from me: "What should I do for Christ?" It has its climax in the "shame of the recreant knight" penetrated by this fresh call of his King. This is exactly as Inigo experienced it, when he looked back upon the "First Week" of his past sinful life and resolved then and there, like St. Francis, to become a new man for whom the bitter would be sweet in Christ. Therefore the profoundly theological "history of sin," proceeding from the fall of the angels to that of our first parents, foreshadows in outline what the meditation on the Two Standards reveals in full: that "the regulating of our daily life," a keynote of the Exercises, means a battle to a decision between Christ and Satan.

Thus, the Spiritual Exercises, which are arranged with a view to the election of a state of life, stand or fall with this Christological foundation. Only by holding fast to this view do we gain a solid vantage point for manifold practical questions, such as those mooted by the oldest directories and even by Ignatius himself.[63] They might be questions such as the following: To whom are the Exercises in their entirety to be given? Are three-day retreats, comprising only meditations of the First Week, to be labelled "Spiritual Exercises" at all? Is the Second Week, together with the contemplation on the Kingdom of Christ, to be "tacked on" in these three-day retreats; if they are, to what extent and with what object in view? An unequivocal answer to these questions is supplied by the eighteenth annotation of the Exercises and, in like manner, by the directories written by Ignatius himself; that is, whatever goes beyond the First Week belongs "to the domain of the election" and should therefore be given to the exercitant only if grace and aptitude enable him to profit from it. Ignatius and his first companions viewed with suspicion any attempt "to water down" the substance of the Spiritual Exercises.

Conversely, from all we have said, the statement also holds good that if the First Week be conceived Christologically it may act as a sufficient substitute for the omis-

sion of the Second Week, especially a Second Week
hurriedly dragged in at the last moment and never permitted to wield its full effect. It is much better to adhere
to the rule that Ignatius dictated to Polanco: "If those
who are to make the Spiritual Exercises are not prepared
spiritually, so as to give promise of drawing greater spiritual fruit from them, the retreat master should be content with giving them the First Week only, dismissing
them with a certain thirst for spiritual things and putting
them off till they show more tangible signs that greater
spiritual fruit may be expected of them." [64]

The second result of our historical investigations into
the primitive origins of the substance of the Spiritual
Exercises is that we are *de facto* in a better position to
fill out the parable of the two kings in the contemplation
on the Kingdom of Christ in the vivid sense that Ignatius
attributed to it. It is well known that a vast amount of
historical material has been assembled on this subject,
beginning with the crusades and wars against the Moors
and ending with the expedition of Charles V against
Tunis and the naval plan of Ignatius himself. [65] From an
historical point of view, our method would be more accurate if we concentrated upon the idea of a king found
in the introduction to the Spanish edition of Ludolph of
Saxony's life of Christ, which also runs through the entire work of Jacopo de Voragine, and then correlated
these elements with the ideals that animated Inigo as a
page and as a soldier. For this is precisely the source
from which proceeded the contemplation on the Kingdom of Christ, or, to speak more accurately, the source
by which the mystical grace of Manresa could establish

a nexus, thus enabling Inigo to arrive at the theological
idea of the Kingdom of Christ as expressed by the words
of the Church drawn from Holy Writ: "Be brave in
battle, fight with the ancient serpent, and you will receive an eternal kingdom" (Antiphon of the *Magnificat*
in the Second Vespers of the *Commune Apostolorum*).

From all this we gain a deeper insight into the nature
of the ideal of perfection which Ignatius desired to see
incorporated in his "Company." The earliest form of his
Order begins to appear for him in that part of the Spiritual Exercises where, at the end of the meditation on
the Two Standards, he begs "to be received under the
standard of his Lord in the highest spiritual poverty,
thereby to imitate Him better" (no. 147). Indeed, it is
by means of the discernment of spirits, intensified by the
deeply moving sight of the army camps portraying the
history of the world, that the choice and character of a
state of life is brought about. Hence the spiritual guide,
whom we usually style "retreat master," should be an
expert in discerning the "subtle and advanced" things of
the spiritual life (no. 9), a man who knows how to distinguish different spirits in himself and in others, with a
sure and light touch. That is the sense of those annotations which Ignatius, with sublime prudence, prefixed
to his Spiritual Exercises ("Introductory Observations,"
6–15). But in these annotations he merely sketches the
ideal that he wishes to see realized by his co-laborers in
the Society of Jesus. In a passage of his Directory, Ignatius, giving the obverse of the above idea, makes the
following remark: "The more a person seems suited to
embrace the manner of life in the Society of Jesus, the

more suited he is, generally speaking, to make the whole
of the Exercises." [66] The Jesuit, formed by the Spiritual
Exercises, should consequently be adept in the discernment of spirits, a man of "discretion"—with all that is
implied in this really untranslatable term which is so
closely connected with the "discernment of spirits," *discretio spirituum*. Again and again Ignatius speaks of this
quality in his Constitutions. He demands this "discretion" from candidates who wish to join his Order; at a
minimum, it is that capacity for spiritual formation
which may be described as tact, a calmly sober readiness
in regard to decisions of practical life (*discretio in rebus
agendis*). He looked upon "indiscreet devotions" as
almost an impediment to entrance into the Society of
Jesus.[67]

What is here outlined as a minimum for beginners is
amplified in the qualifications demanded by Ignatius in
a general of the Order: he must be a man full of "discreet" prudence in matters pertaining to the interior life
and to the handling of men.[68] His contemporaries were
right in asserting that in drawing this portrait of the general, Ignatius was simply drawing a portrait of himself.[69]
Above all, this "discretion" has reference to the "difficult" works of prayer, penance, and obedience. It is
needed wherever there is question of important matters
in the Kingdom of God and wherever a critical decision
has to be made. It is a front-line virtue where Christ and
Belial, light and darkness, stand face to face and where
it is necessary to unmask "the angels of light" as the
widely dispersed emissaries of the "throne" of Babylon
"made up of fire and smoke." The primitive form in

which the spiritual life appeared to Inigo at the commencement of his conversion, the substance of the original cell of the Spiritual Exercises, so to speak, that is
what should be for every Jesuit the source of ever-
advancing knowledge and progress. The Jesuit ought to
be "a divine weather-prophet," with a keen sense of
what is divine and diabolical in the events of universal
history. He should be a man who knows his Jerusalem
and Babylon thoroughly. This is the whole purport of
the petition in the Two Standards where the exercitant
asks for some introduction to the "intentions" and designs of Christ our Lord and those of the enemy of
human nature (no. 135), and begs again and again
"for knowledge of the deceits of the rebel chief and for
knowledge of the true life exemplified in the sovereign
and true Commander" (no. 139).

In this ability to discern spirits lies concealed that fine
interior sureness of mind that we call discretion. Here we
touch upon a bit of the Ignatian ideal of perfection that
has so often and on various occasions been thrown up
to the Society as a bit of Jesuitical cunning, "hiding itself," as Fülop-Miller words it, "under a thousand
masks." Indeed, it was a daring attempt on the part of
Ignatius to formulate in set rules this inconceivable attitude, so to speak, and to demand their observance from
a Society that was constantly growing. No one can have
a right understanding or make an unfailingly correct use
of this discretion, except one who has from prayerful experience learned to know the source from which it
springs: that is, from knowledge, enlightened by grace,
of the discernment of spirits, or, to speak theologically,

from knowledge of the relation existing between nature
and grace, between Christ and the world. It is only by
taking into consideration such a discretion that we can
understand how Inigo, even during his first still raw beginnings, was being prepared for the bold stroke of
founding a new order which is to unite two disparate
elements: (1) an entire renunciation of the world by its
members through a total and unreserved offering of
themselves to Christ the King; and (2) a commingling
of the members with the world they have given up in
order to wrest it from the control of Satan. Only by
means of this "divine discretion" is it possible for a soldier of this Company to move along the thin and almost
invisible frontline which passes through the world and
the center of his own heart. It is always a hazard for
anyone, even one with a keen scent for the movements
of the spirit, to be in the world but not of the world.
Who will dare to maintain that the sons of Ignatius were
always successful in evading this danger? Who, on the
other hand, because some have failed, will refuse to mix
boldly with the world in order to snatch it away from
him who has set himself up "as the prince of this world"
(John 12:31; 14:30) and, by such an action, win it
back for Christ and make the kingly rule of Him "who
created this world" (John 1:10) a substantial reality?

If our investigations so far have led us to infer that, in
Inigo's future Order, obedience and discipline were the
result of his descent and breeding, now we find that the
outcome of his encounter with the thought of Christian
tradition makes his attitude stand out with even greater
distinctness. Obedience is now seen to be, not merely "the

regimentation" of a company, not merely a discipline
enforced by the rules of the Society as a necessary pre-
requisite for the apostolic life, but as a wholehearted devotion to a King engaged in constant battle with a Satan
who has flung off the yoke of obedience. Discipline does
not mean merely aristocratic reserve nor the fundamental way of acting which gave birth to the caricature
of the Jesuit as excelling all other men in knowledge,
cunning and power. Discipline is the virtue of a soldier
who is in actual combat with Satan, a soldier who knows
no other way of getting the better of his unscrupulous
and disconcerting foe "with his snares and chains" (no.
142) than by a watchful, cautious, and clear-eyed freedom of spirit. This freedom of spirit, however, springs
from that interior cleanliness, through which a soldier of
Christ preserves his own soul free "from the fire and
smoke of Babylon." It is precisely this clear-visioned
liberty of spirit that is at the root of Ignatian discipline
and its absolute renunciation of all that savors of the
world. Vice versa, it is only discretion again that enables
us to understand why Ignatius sends his sons into a world
full of dangers, into "an everyday life" [70] that apparently
does not call for any "hard and heroic" activity. The
same soldier of the Company who just a little while ago
desired and begged to be enrolled under the banner of
the highest poverty is now bidden to practice it only
"according to the measure of holy discretion." [71] It is
through this discretion alone that we are able to grasp
the fact that the Jesuit approaches the world only from
the remote standpoint of the cross, that there is in him
not so much a mystical running away from the world as

a mystical joy in running toward the world in order to win it back again for his divine Leader, Christ. Like Inigo, the Jesuit travels the road that goes from the heroic cave at Manresa to the fully developed outlook on the world of the Gesu Church at Rome.[72]

In his pilgrimage from his native castle to Montserrat and Manresa, Inigo had only a dim idea of all these things. The clear knowledge and the definitive seal came to him only at Manresa in the powerful mystic light that burst upon him, as it were, "from above." We shall now make it our task to describe what this illumination meant in the formation of his ideal of perfection.

Chapter 3

The Mystical Transformation of St. Ignatius Into a Man of the Church

NEITHER the influence of his early court-and-camp environment, nor his contact with the tradition of Christian perfection, offers a fully satisfactory historical explanation of the fact that Inigo, after a mediocre preparatory schooling in the spiritual life and a brief acquaintance with spiritual things, could become the author of the Spiritual Exercises. When, after his night of vigil at Montserrat, he turned his steps toward the tiny hamlet of Manresa, he had not the least inkling of what was to happen to him there. Tucked away in his heart were the experiences he had passed through in his tussle with the spirits at Loyola—which, sad to say, gave birth only to strangely extravagant resolutions; and tucked away in a pocket of his rough sackcloth garment was the volume of extracts he had copied out in vari-colored inks, and which he read and reread again and again. "He turned off to a little town called Manresa. Here he determined to remain a few days at the hospital and to add a few notes to his scrapbook, which for his consolation he constantly carried about with him and carefully guarded during the course of his pilgrimage." [73] The "few days" stretched out into ten months; the book of excerpts turned into the book of the Spiritual Exercises; the pilgrim blossomed out into the mystic; the former knight was changed into "a new man" who received those flashes of illumination which drove him on to the founding of a new order. What, we may wonder, actually did take place at Manresa?

The only possible answer is that at Manresa occurred God's mystical invasion into the soul of Inigo, conquering all opposition, linking together all Inigo's previous spiritual experiences, yet at the same time sovereignly transcending them with the object of making him, as he acknowledges in his autobiography, "a new soldier of Christ," a man of the Church. [74] All this was accomplished by means of spiritual exercises. During this period at Manresa these exercises took on in his soul—searchlighted by mystic supernatural illumination—that peculiar structure of knowledge from which the Society of Jesus was formed. Because of this, Ignatius enters the ranks of those great men in the history of the Church who were raised up by God at critical times in the spiritual battle between Christ and Satan. That "discernment of spirits" which they had first learned from experience within their own souls they extended to the decision which is always being made amidst the struggles of the Church militant. These men confine the spirit to the limits of the visible Church and thereby secure its possession for the body of the Christ struggling here below.

From the inclusion of Ignatius in the noble line of these
great men there follow the last and most fundamental
conclusions for the understanding of the ideal of perfection which St. Ignatius wanted to see embodied in the
Exercises and hence also in his "Company."

Three things therefore call for comment here: first,
how the mysticism of Manresa influenced the ideal of the
Spiritual Exercises; second, the placing of St. Ignatius on
an equal footing with the great men of the Church, a
fact capable of historical demonstration; finally, the
consequences flowing from the two preceding facts concerning the ideals of the Spiritual Exercises and of the
Society of Jesus.

1. The Mysticism of Manresa

Ignatius himself and all his intimates stressed again
and again the fact that the Spiritual Exercises had their
origin in the solitude of Manresa and that, consequently,
as far as the essentials are concerned, nothing existed before that time and nothing was added to it afterwards,
despite all the additions and corrections made by Ignatius
over a long period of years. They emphasized, besides,
that it was God Himself who inspired him. We have it
from the lips of Ignatius "that God was the schoolmaster
and Inigo the pupil, untrained and backward." [75] Nadal
states that the Spiritual Exercises came into being
"through God's grace and inspiration." [76] According to
the testimony of Polanco, "Ignatius received the Spiritual Exercises taught by God Himself." [77] Laynez in his
earliest biography of Ignatius is the plainest witness of

all. He says: "At Manresa Inigo was strengthened, taught, and illumined by His Divine Majesty in a wholly singular manner. As a consequence he began to look at the things of God with entirely different eyes, to distinguish and test the different spirits, to relish interiorly divine things and to impart them to his neighbor with the same simplicity and love with which he himself had received them." [78]

The emphatic underscoring of these words, "God alone," can have only one meaning when considered in reference to that mystical grace which, as Ignatius himself phrases it, turned the Manresan pilgrim "into a new man with a new intellect." [79] The mystical action wiped out, so to speak, all that preceded; it was as if his "slow-thinking mind had been removed altogether and his heart could only cry out in astonishment: 'What strange life is this that I am now beginning to live?'" [80]

Thanks to the clear data Ignatius gives, it is possible even at this late date to reconstruct exactly the structure and progressive perfecting of this mystical illumination. This reconstruction also shows us the basic outline of the edifice of the Spiritual Exercises as it rises architectonically.

We are able to mark clearly three stages in the mystical evolution of the Manresa penitent: the quiet beginning period, the mystic "night of the soul," and the period of Trinitarian visions. The distinguishing feature of the first of these periods was, according to Ignatius' own testimony, "a mood of great equanimity coupled with abundant joy, without, however, any clear knowledge at all of the interior spiritual life." [81] He means by this that he has as yet no acquaintance with mystical graces. He tells us about one phenomenon only: often he saw in broad daylight "something" like a serpent with many eyes, and he derived much consolation and joy from the sight.[82] Somewhat later we learn from him "that he had marvelous illuminations and extraordinary spiritual consolations." [83] These, he found in the end, had a diabolic significance. Just as at Loyola, he is still at this time in the period of "the discernment of the spirits."

The second period is replete with the most frightful sufferings of soul, even to the thought of committing suicide; there were violent attempts to regain his former grace and peace of soul by fasting, depriving himself of sleep, and praying for seven hours daily.

Only after this does the third decisive period of the actual mystical graces set in. Ignatius has described this period in his autobiography in a systematic sort of digression that indeed interrupts the continuity of the running narrative, but certainly not in such a way that the facts narrated run counter to the historical sequence of events. At the commencement of this stage, Ignatius seemed to himself like a man "who has been awakened from a drugged sleep." [84] Divinely bright sunlight shone into his soul. The long retreat had begun for him.

This first vision which Ignatius mentions is that of the Blessed Trinity. God Himself is the object of it. "So strong was the impression made upon him that it was never erased from his memory the rest of his life and that henceforth he felt a great devotion to the divine majesty whenever he prayed to the Blessed Trinity." [85]

From that day devotion to the Blessed Trinity is the distinguishing mark of his spirituality.

He also mystically beheld how all things in creation proceeded from the triune God. The idea of creation was brought home to him. "With great spiritual joy the manner in which God created the world is represented to him." [86] From that day on he can meditate about all "the other things on the face of the earth" only in the light of their proceeding from and returning to God (no. 23). The vision also revealed to him that Christ is "the Eternal Lord of all things" (no. 98).

In this way the mystical vision of the humanity of Christ drops into its proper niche and he sees this humanity in such a manner that a sharp distinction is drawn between the form in which Christ appeared on earth and His sacramental presence in the Mystical Body of the Church.

If, in studying the content and manner of this mystical guiding of Inigo, we have already sketched the outlines of the Spiritual Exercises, these outlines are now filled in with the definitely molded substance of the Exercises through the medium of the greatest and last grace conferred upon Inigo at Manresa—namely, the "great illumination" obtained in his vision on the banks of the river Cardoner near the chapel of St. Paul.

The hour of this vision marks the real birth of the Spiritual Exercises. In it, all the iron filings (that is, all the scattered materials of his previously acquired spiritual knowledge) were gathered up by the magnetic force of a wholly new burst of illumination into an organic whole—an organic whole which we call the Exercises, their theology and their supernatural psychology, where everything has its proper place in relation to God. Ignatius himself is witness to the well-nigh overwhelming impression made upon him by this vision: "The eyes of his spirit were opened, not so much in the sense of his seeing a vision, but in that he was given to understand with certainty a multitude of things, some concerning the spiritual life only, some concerning faith and human wisdom. All this was accompanied by such a flood of light that all appeared entirely new to him." [87] He adds that this one "great illumination" did more for him than all the graces taken together which he had received during the previous sixty-two years of his life. In narrating the astounding impression which this vision made upon him, Ignatius lays less stress on the content of the vision than upon its personal effect. But we know from the testimony of Ignatius and his familiars that the primary effect of the vision was the shaping of the Spiritual Exercises.

Elsewhere Ignatius tells us, "I saw, felt in my interior, and penetrated with my mind all the mysteries of the Catholic Faith." [88] With these words he points out to us what the fundamental grace of this vision was: the "synthetic" view (to use an epithet coined by Father Leturia) [89] which it gave him of the connection between all the truths of divine revelation, of the relation of all things to the majesty of the Blessed Trinity, and of how all this is contained in Christ, in the struggle between the spirits, and, finally, in the Church. This is explicitly affirmed by Polanco in his life of St. Ignatius:

One day he went from Manresa to a certain chapel situated about a thousand paces away; and, as he sat down near the bank of a river, his soul was suddenly and extraordinarily illuminated by a flood of light.

He saw in a marvelous manner into the divine mysteries. This light was extended also to the power of discernment between good and evil spirits, and was so overwhelming that he beheld, so it seemed to him, all human and divine things with wholly new eyes of the spirit. . . . Thereupon he set himself to devise a plan or method for purifying the soul from its sins by contrition and confession, for meditating on the life of Christ and making a right election of a state of life and of all other things, and for progressing in everything which tended to inflame the soul more and more with love of God. In this way he created a little book of very great profit for the salvation of his neighbor.[90]

To the citations quoted above we may add the statement of Father Nadal in which he narrates the further and more accurate particulars concerning the striking effect exercised by this vision upon the final shaping of the Spiritual Exercises:

During Ignatius' sojourn at Manresa, God gave him a most profound insight into, and feeling for, the mysteries of our holy Faith and the Catholic Church. At that time also He inspired him with the Spiritual Exercises by moving him to devote himself entirely to the service of God and the salvation of souls. He revealed to him this purpose, especially and in the most signal manner, in the meditation on the Kingdom of Christ and the Two Standards. Inigo saw in this his life-aim, the goal to which he must give himself wholly and which he must ever keep before his mind in all his undertakings. . . . This life-aim is the same as that which the Society of Jesus still professes at the present time.[91]

This wholly new mind coordinated the truths which it already possessed into the total structure of the Spiritual Exercises:

The inner ways, heading as it were toward distant horizons and without any fixed direction, are now definitely marked out and automatically fall into their proper place and order. The "purgative life" occupies its fundamental position; the mysteries of the life of Christ are given their characteristic features; the discernment of spirits (and the choice of a state of life linked with it) is consciously shifted to the center of all spiritual activity, and the whole is then crowned with the contemplation for attaining the love of God. Above all, the ideal of the King and the Two Standards, with which Inigo was already familiar even before this date, takes on a wholly new meaning in the whole of this constructive refashioning of the Spiritual Exercises. At Loyola he saw in Christ the eternal King only a model for imitation, and the example of His great-hearted sufferings evoked loving sympathy in him as it did in the saints all down the centuries. But now this King became for him a living person, actively exerting His influence today and yesterday, with the mission entrusted to Him by His Father not yet wholly completed, and seeking therefore, today and yesterday, for generous co-fighters and friends desirous of showing themselves faithful companions in arms.[92]

Here therefore takes place the conversion of Inigo from a merely interior man into an apostle. His terrifying zeal for penance takes a new direction, turning from a merely self-centered consideration of sin to a history of sin in its relation to all the other mysteries of our holy Faith, a history of sin passing from the fall of Lucifer to the most delicate discernment of spirits in the souls of men. The sympathetic meditation on the life of Christ, drawn from Ludolph of Saxony's work and entered in red ink into his copybook, now shifts to the mysteries of the life of Christ built up with inexorable logic to the climax of the election. This, precisely, is the radical distinction between Ignatius and the "modern devotion" (of the Brothers of the Common Life). Ignatius at Manresa fashioned their formless "Imitation of Jesus," completely changing it to the following of Christ present in the Church. "The Kingdom of Christ is the Church, and in her all the other mysteries coalesce." At the central point of the Exercises, the election, Ignatius points to the "hierarchical Church, our holy Mother" as the supreme criterion for the discernment of spirits (no. 170). The Church herself is the touchstone for every genuine and "true attitude of mind which we ought to have in the Church militant" (no. 352). God, Church, and obedience: these now form the triad by which Ignatius measures all ethical values. Nadal, therefore, is justified in saying that the vision by the river Cardoner gave Ignatius the most vivid insight "into the divine mysteries and into the Church." Briefly, if we look at the Exercises thus given their final shape and form, we are compelled to say that by the mystical transformation which took place at Manresa, Ignatius, the pilgrim and the penitent, was made over into the man of the Church (*l'homme d'Eglise*).

By attending to the formal element in this transformation, it is possible to demonstrate this statement even more exactly. Hitherto the unlimitedness of his "more" had displayed itself by almost suicidal attempts in the prac-

tice of rigorous penances and by flitting dreams of entering a Carthusian monastery or making barefooted pilgrimages. Now this limitless "more," by the power of the
Manresan mysticism, is curbed within the limits of the
visible Kingdom of Christ, within the Church, even
within the bounds of reasonableness itself.

In the first place, it is most interesting to note precisely
where in his autobiography Ignatius speaks of this breaking in of mystical wisdom. He states explicitly that the
abandonment of his rigorous penances was the consequence of the illuminations received at Manresa and of
his turning toward the salvation of souls, that is, of his
turning toward the Church. "When he had begun to be
consoled by God and when he noticed the great fruits
which he gained in souls by spiritual direction, he stopped
practicing those immoderate penances he had formerly
indulged in; he began again to cut his fingernails and
hair." [93]

Secondly, "this conforming to the more common life"
was guided by the new ideal derived from the mystical
illumination "of the modest and amiable leader" sending
his messengers to all parts of the world, of the King in
the Church militant. Henceforth his purpose is to aid the
souls of other men.

From now on, the "social moment" [94] in the meditation of the Two Standards, which is at the same time the
dynamic element in the picture of Christ, occupied Ignatius' whole mind, and everything else had to be subordinated to this new ideal of service. At the conclusion
of his account concerning all the mystical favors received
at Manresa, Ignatius adds the following words: "I had

a lively desire to converse about divine things and to find
people who were capable of holding such a conversa-
tion." [95] His original plan of pilgrimaging to Jerusalem
as a penitent is changed into a plan of apostolic ministry: "Over and above satisfying his own personal devotion in the Holy Land, he desired also to help souls." [96]
Moreover the first narratives of his intimates never omit
to mention that the origin of his apostolic ideal, to which
his ideal of perfection was to conform itself in the future,
was an essential fruit of the mystical graces conferred on
him near the river Cardoner. Laynez notes, "Simul-
taneously (with the graces to which the Exercises owe
their existence) at Manresa he turned to the promotion
of the salvation of souls." [97] "Using what he had experienced in his own soul," says Polanco, "he now desired
to aid other souls." [98] And Nadal comments, "At the
very moment he felt the total self-surrender of his soul
become a living reality through these Exercises, he was
drawn and driven to devote himself utterly to the care
of the salvation of souls." [99] This service of the Divine
Majesty became synonymous with the helping of souls,
work to be done within the Church militant; and this
again was tantamount to his plan of gathering about
him suitable men who should follow out in their lives
the same ideal of service. The vision on the Cardoner
River marks the beginning (as we shall show later on) of
the plan for founding a "company"; it also marks the
passage from the merely personal to the ecclesiastical,
from Onuphrius to the Apostles, from mystical absorp-
tion to the study of Latin at Barcelona, from the grey
sackcloth garment to the soutane, from living on herbs

to the routine of the "common life," from the pilgrim to the respected priest, from the concentration on the interior of the Ludolphian "modern devotion" to the militant Christ fighting in the militant Church and calling for recruits here and now. Thus the Church becomes for him the rule for measuring enthusiasm. On the river Cardoner was born the Ignatian "discretion of love." Ignatius was to write many years later: "Every internal experience that comes directly from God must be in humble harmony with the prescriptions of the Church and with obedience." [100] For since the first Pentecost, the spirit of Christ which is poured out upon all flesh operates only in the visible Church. "The same spirit that dwells in Christ the bridegroom and in the Church His bride, also leads and guides us to the salvation of our souls; and our holy Mother the Church is led and guided by the same spirit that gave us the ten commandments." [101]

2. Ignatius Ranks with Men of the Church

By reason of his turning toward the Church, a process completed in all essentials by the mystic graces of Manresa, St. Ignatius joins the ranks of the great churchmen whom God has raised up at critical times in the long history of the Church to fend off the danger of a too one-sided spiritualization of Christian revelation and perfection. The connection between all these men is far beyond mere literary dependence and, hence, is incapable of being fitted into the categories of history based directly on sources. This connection is, so to speak, meta-historical, founded on an identity of mystical insight which inspires them, removed from each other though they are in time and space and separated from one another as to historical sources, and on an identity of fundamental ideas, which in turn are then expressed in surprisingly parallel principles.

From this long line of great men we shall select the names of a few figures who are the true ancestors of Ignatius in a much more profound sense than Ludolph of Saxony, Jacopo de Voragine, or Thomas a Kempis. All these men were called by mystical grace to intervene at critical moments in the great spiritual battle being waged down the centuries between Satan and Christ living in His Church. They always appeared where the subtlest and most diabolical danger loomed; where Lucifer, who had been created one of the noblest spirits of God, appearing as an angel of light, has counterfeited the humble, visible work of Christ by the unlimited "more" of his "inspirations." Such a crisis occurred when Greek Gnosticism raised its proud head, when the mystic spirituality of Neo-Platonism together with Egyptian monasticism threatened the very life of the hierarchical Church, and finally when the detached interiority (quietism) of medieval mysticism began to doubt the need of a visible Church, which had at that time been torn asunder and become too "human."

A. IGNATIUS OF ANTIOCH

To meet the deadly danger of Gnosticism, God called Ignatius of Antioch. Ignatius of Loyola sensed, so to speak, his spiritual affinity with this man of the early Church when, in honor of this Saint, he changed his name from Inigo to Ignatius and in one of his letters styled him "that glorious Saint for whom I have in our Lord, or wish to have, a very special reverential devotion." [102] He was familiar with him from the pages of *The Golden Legend;* especially was he familiar with that saying of his, taken from St. Paul's Epistle to the Romans, "My love is crucified." This saying he later placed at the head of his maxims,[103] because for him it had the same meaning as his own "discreet love." Love is true love when it is a crucified love; inspiration is true inspiration when it is measured by the humanity of Christ. This principle is basic to the discernment of spirits in primitive Christianity as it was formulated by Ignatius of Antioch.

The primitive Church from the first moment of its birth, so to speak, was compelled to be on its guard against the "spirit." One need only think of the instructions found in the pastoral epistles of St. Paul, or those contained in the *Didache,* where the discernment of spirits receives expression for the first time in the classical apothegm: "Not everyone who speaks in the spirit is a prophet, but only he who resembles Christ in his manner of life." [104] The genuineness of all mystical gifts is therefore measured by their likeness to the humble life of the Incarnate Word. The same teaching is found in *Pastor Hermas.* The genuine spirit of mysticism (mystical grace) which comes "from above" and not "from below" (that is, not from nature and the devil) moves men to fit themselves into the Church calmly, silently, and humbly.[105]

These questions became almost burning when Gnosticism began to exercise its pernicious influence. A search through the letters of Ignatius of Antioch gives us the following data: the Gnostics were "spiritual" Christians who, with genuine Greek subtlety, could not understand how it was possible for God to redeem us in a form that was truly human by a bloody death on the cross.[106] Hence they held themselves proudly aloof from the other Christians and came together for the celebration of their Eucharistic service, not in the common place of assembly, but in private conventicles; their Eucharistic services were for them a spiritual (and not a fleshly, material) sacrifice of the Body and Blood of Christ.[107] Finally, fraternal charity was beyond their comprehension, that charity which is the distinguishing mark of the genuine and visible Church made one by the Blood of Christ.[108]

In opposition to all these tenets and practices, Ignatius of Antioch set up his teaching. In his case, as in that of Ignatius of Loyola many centuries later,[109] his teaching had its source in a "noble" and burning soul, in mystical illumination. The Ignatius of long ago had beheld in a vision "celestial things and the thrones of the angels" [110] and had heard from the "Spirit" mysterious words.[111] But he measured the genuineness of this gift by the humble self-restraint he imposed upon himself and by the impulse to embrace the cross of the man Jesus.[112] It was from this experience of real discernment of spirits that the teaching of this Father of the Church was derived. We can sum it up in two basic propositions: the tendency of the genuine spirit is to assimilate men to the man Christ and to obey the humanly visible Church;

the visibility of the cross and of the Church therefore
must be surety for invisible things.

The spirit and the cross—their deep theological foundation lies in the fact that in God's plan of salvation the
cross of Christ holds the central place in all that happens
in the natural world, even of all that happens in the
supernatural world. "Let no one deceive himself—even
the heavenly powers and the majesty of angels, the visible and invisible principalities must face damnation if
they refuse to believe in the Blood of Christ. Let him
grasp it who can!" [113] This is exactly the same thought
that permeates the whole book of the Spiritual Exercises,
where Ignatius divides rational creatures according to
the position they take in relation to the Incarnate Word
(no. 71). In the vision on the river Cardoner he saw the
interrelation of the mysteries of our holy Faith, from the
sin of the angels to the colloquy with our crucified
Saviour (no. 53). The cross is also the deciding factor in
the election. The "spirit" drives toward assimilation with
the crucified Christ. This is exactly what took place long
before in the case of the first Ignatius. The true spirit
inclines men toward imitation of "the Passion of
God," [114] toward imitation of our "insulted, robbed, and
contemned Lord." [115] The spirit that does not do this is
"sown by the devil," [116] is a "proud spirit"; [117] its hidden
falseness is revealed by "whether it puts forth branches
of the cross or not." [118] Because of this theological doctrine, Ignatius of Antioch is the father of the anti-Gnostic
discernment of spirits as it was later brought to mature
development by Irenaeus, that other great man of the
Church.

Spirit and Church: that is the other idea reiterated with passionate insistence in the letters of Ignatius of Antioch. The motion of the true spirit always urges toward obedience to the hierarchical Church—for there is no unity with the Father except through Christ; no unity with Christ except through the bishop. This is the revelation given Ignatius of Antioch by the spirit that "moves as it wills" in him: "I stood in the midst of the assembly of the faithful and cried with a ringing voice: 'Cleave to your bishop, your priests and deacons.' And the spirit revealed to me: 'Do nothing contrary to the orders of your bishop,' become imitators of Christ as He Himself was an imitator of His Father." [119] The theological grounds for this way of acting are again clear: the triad—Father, Christ, bishop—has become for Ignatius of Antioch almost the whole substance of God's plan of salvation in relation to the new man, Jesus Christ.[120] Consequently, for him the Church stands as the bulwark upon which the whole might of Satan is shattered and broken.[121] She is the bride of Christ, anointed with the perfumes of immortality and dispelling "the foul smell of Satan." [122] But this is identical with the results gained from the Manresan mysticism, beginning with the rules for thinking rightly with the Church down to, and including, the letters of St. Ignatius of Loyola; time and again he reiterates that every spirit is to be measured by the humble visibility of the Church of the Crucified and by obedience to its commandments, which originate from the same spirit as that which operates in our interior.[123]

From all we have learned, the ideal of perfection in

the Spiritual Exercises may be defined as follows: "A
fresh ordering of life by means of assimilation to God,
who stooped down to us in the Incarnation and died for
us on the cross; an ordering of life accomplished through
the fight with Satan, which will go on in the Church till
the final destruction of the kingdom set up by the 'chief
of the enemies.' This end is achieved most perfectly by
the display of an undaunted readiness to serve, which, in
turn, shows itself as genuine by cultivating the right disposition in regard to the Church militant." But these are
exactly the principles of perfection expressed long ago by
Ignatius of Antioch. Our way of ascent lies through
obedience to the Church which is made visible in her
bishops and through battle with the prince of this world,
unto the homecoming in God by newness of life through
Christ. "Hold fast to the bishop, in order that God may
hold fast to you. I will wager my soul on those who are
obedient to the bishop, the priests, and deacons. Toil with
one another, fight, run, suffer, rest, keep vigils with one
another; and in this way gain the approval of the military leader from whom you receive your pay. Let none
of you turn deserter." [124] "It is certain from the days
when God manifested Himself in human form, in order
to bring about the newness of life, that the ancient kingdom of the prince of this world was to be destroyed." [125]

We now see the reason why the new Ignatius was so
fond of his patron's motto: "My love is crucified," [126]
and why he could never forget that other detail he had
read in *The Golden Legend*—that when the Roman
henchmen tore out the heart of Ignatius, they found
IHS inscribed on it in golden letters.[127] As Ribadeneira

tells us, Ignatius of Loyola chose this emblem as the seal
and blazon of his Company [128] out of reverence for the
Ignatius of the early Christian times. "His heart, like
that of the ancient Ignatius, burned with love for the
holy name of Jesus. Our Holy Father Ignatius wished to
resemble this other Ignatius not merely by similarity of
name but much more by similarity of life." [129]

B. BASIL, BENEDICT, AND AUGUSTINE

The second deadly peril to which the ancient Church
was exposed, I should like to designate by the term
"monachism." By this word is meant the tendency into
which the flourishing spiritual movement of Egyptian
monasticism fell toward the close of the fourth century,
because it would not allow the "more" of "its enthusiasm" to be confined by humble service in the visible
Church. This state of affairs was brought about by two
causes: first, the *external* estrangement of Egyptian
monasticism from the Church on the part of both hermits
and the densely crowded, enormous Pachomian convents, whose communities were made up of pious but
often very capricious monks, to a large extent hostile to
the episcopal hierarchy. The second cause was *internal*
seclusion from the Church, a matter of even greater
peril and a disease which Egyptian monasticism con-
tracted as soon as its monasteries were filled, not by
simple Egyptian peasants, but by subtle Greek scholars
from Alexandria and Asia Minor. That situation made
it possible to effect a union on the one hand, between
the theological speculations of Origen and the Neo-

Platonic thirst for a disembodied spirituality, and, on the other, the ascetic ideal of indifference, which was the final object of the monks' striving. Thus, these united streams rushed down in full flood against the humble visibility of the human Christ and his Church in order to sweep away whatever was not "pure" spirit.

It was St. Basil in the East and St. Benedict in the West who fitted this unbalanced "more" of monastic enthusiasm into the framework of the visible Church. Centuries later, while Ignatius was writing his own Constitutions and at the same time humbly measuring his own internal spiritual experiences by the example of the saints, he attentively read the Rule of St. Basil (in the translation by Rufinus) and the Rule of St. Benedict.[130] The Constitutions show traces of both of these Rules. But over and above this external connection, Basil and Ignatius manifest a deeply spiritual kinship with each other by their special talent, springing from mystical depths, for the discernment of spirits in the Church militant. We shall show this deeper connection between the two saints by sketching a few traits they have in common.

To begin with the natural foundation, Basil has given us in the few sure strokes of a letter a description of the whole process of his conversion. Just as for St. Ignatius there had been the vanity of a knightly life, so for St. Basil there had been the vanity of striving after the learning of a typical Greek man. Basil wrote, "I gave much time to vain things and wasted almost the whole time of my youth in a vain endeavor to acquire the knowledge and wisdom which God has declared to be foolish." [131] Ignatius wrote, "Up to the twenty-sixth year of my life

I was given to the vanities of the world." Basil then goes on to say, "Finally I awoke as from a deep sleep, turned my eyes toward the marvelous light of the gospel, bewailed my sins and prayed for light to guide me into an understanding of the truths of the gospel; but above all I strove to amend my life." That was, so to speak, the Manresa of St. Basil; he too retired into the solitude of far-off Egypt. When Ignatius' life had undergone a complete transformation under the power of those first mystical graces at Manresa, he also wrote, "I was like a man roused from heavy slumber." It is the eternally identical process of conversion to God, appearing at the start as an intensified interior life and an attraction toward solitude and a way of life such as that of Onuphrius. Basil made a hermitage in his native Cappadocia and found among the ascetically emaciated followers of Eustathius of Sebaste his long-desired and well-beloved models. For a moment St. Basil in his monastic home on the river Iris was apparently swept along by the main current of the headlong flood waters of monachism. Eustathius was a frequent visitor; they read and gathered excerpts for the *Philokalia;* they admired Origen; Evagrius Pontikus, the future theologian of the tendency toward over-spiritualization, became his disciple and friend. Their craving for severe penances and their unsparing rigor in the treatment of the body were insatiable. As a consequence, Basil, like Ignatius of Loyola later, bore away from his "Manresa" a lifelong, vexing stomach complaint.[132]

Subsequent to this first conversion, there was for Basil, just as for Ignatius, a second conversion, as it were, to the visible, militant Church. Basil was not content to re-

main in luxurious idleness during the stormy days when
a triumphant Arianism reigned almost supreme over the
whole of the then known world (just as Ignatius was not
content during the upheaval of the Reformation to remain hidden and inactive in his beloved solitude). He
became a priest and a theologian, and shortly after a
bishop—one of the staunchest defenders of the visible
and hierarchical Church. Basil was prepared for this
phase during that period when long and painful experience in handling others forced him to compose his
great ascetical lifework, the Rule and its explanatory
instructions. From the extravagant "spirituality" of his
disciple Evagrius, he learned the danger into which
monasticism (or monachism) could fall.[133] The only
guarantee for genuineness of spirit and enthusiasm, it
seemed to him, lay in such restrictions upon the ideal of
the monk as he had laid down in his Rule; namely, in
the incorporation of monasticism into the body of the
visible Church, and in obedience to the cenobitical way
of life tempered to a noble reserve. Through his associa-
tion with his former friend, Eustathius, he came to know
what we may call "rules for thinking rightly with the
Church"; he described, in the letter mentioned above,
how this community of monks wearing "humble habits
and rough garments," became through their spiritual
pride the storm center of an heretical movement hostile
to the hierarchical Church. The authenticity or spurious-
ness of the Eustathian inspiration is to be judged by its
attitude toward obedience, properly constituted authority
in the Church, and the directions of Pope Liberius in
Rome. The same tendency that influenced Evagrius in a

speculative theological question was at work in Eustathius in a matter of Church discipline. They thought that for men "of high spirituality," the Church was merely a transition stage, something still material; even the humanity of Christ and the humble form of a servant which He assumed were to be looked upon in this way. These two concepts eluded the grasp of the subtle Greek mind. Basil broke with Eustathius and Evagrius, and from then on his whole life was characterized by a passionate devotion—combined with, and regulated by, prudence—to the humble work of the man Jesus.

This double trait is seen primarily in his work as a bishop. For him the visible Church is the only place where "God is adored in truth"; everything else is "mere private assembly." "Away with private churches and synagogues," he cries in one of his homilies.[134] The theological reason for his view he indicates in the treatise *De Spiritu Sancto*.[135] The Holy Ghost has only one efficient purpose: He prepares the flesh of Jesus in the womb of the Virgin; that is why He descends upon the humble man Jesus standing in the river Jordan and drives Him on to fight with Satan in the desert; that is why He raises Him from the dead on the first Easter Sunday; finally, that is why He now works in the Church militant. There is the paradox: that in the humility of the Incarnation and the death on the cross the Godhead is revealed in an entirely different light from that in a purely spiritual conception.[136] In the last analysis, the "mystery of the Church" is the truth of the real and entire body of Christ.[137] The Church is that body.[138]

The same theological teaching also permeates Basil's

work as a monk. As he points out in the seventh of his "more explicit rules" (a basic one for all future times), monastic life, for Basil, is not the subjective individuality of the hermit, however lofty that may be. The ultimate reason for his position lies in the theological doctrine of the Church as the Body of Christ and in the immediate consequence of this doctrine: that the Church is a community welded together by the bond of humble fraternal charity.[139]

For this ecclesiastical community, perfection, in the true sense of the word, consists in the imitation of our Saviour. Here St. Basil formulates the principle which is already found stated in the *Didache* and in the writings of St. Ignatius of Antioch. "A Christian's purpose in life is to imitate Christ according to the example He gave us in His human nature and in a manner adapted to each one's state of life."[140] The norm of the spirit is, therefore, the human Christ and the measure of grace conferred upon the individual. Hence, Basil continues, in a religious community a superior should stand before his community as a perfect example of an imitator of Christ, in order that thus he might encourage the weaker members according to the words of the Apostle, "Be imitators of me, as I am of Christ." In a superior such action calls for humility; in a subject, obedience of mind and heart; and detachment from the world essentially consists in obedience. Basil is the real father of the ideal of obedience with a theological substratum—the ideal whose function it is to turn the monk into a "soldier of Christ." Obedience assimilates us to the obedient Christ, obedient even unto death on the cross.[141] For Basil, therefore, obedience takes in the "account of conscience," [142] the regulation of our external conduct by "rules of modesty," [143] even the "discretion" shown in the practice of prayer and penance; [144] for the monk is a man who has entered into the service of the Church militant as a good soldier of Christ, and, in consequence, is battling against Satan, who constantly attacks the Church with his diabolical stratagems and continually casts out his nets to catch souls.[145] Basil's language has almost the ring of Ignatius'. Basil's ideal of Christ the King, his soldierly, courageous following of Christ in labors and the cross, his readiness for service, the pitching of his tent on the public military highway, the entrance into glory—all this he pictures in what we may truly call "a meditation on the Kingdom of Chrst," showing us once again how truly the substance of the Spiritual Exercises belongs to early Christianity.

Excellent are a king's laws for his ordinary subjects, but more kingly and noble are his military orders to his soldiers. As if he were hearing commands of a military nature proclaimed, therefore, let him who longs for heavenly and truly sublime dignities, him who desires to be with Christ eternally, let him be ready to follow when he hears the mighty words: "If any man minister to me, let him follow me; for where I am, there also shall my minister be." Where is Christ our King? In heaven. Thither, therefore, O soldier of Christ, you must hasten your march. A true soldier does not settle down in a fixed abode, does not cling to land and earthly possessions, does not suffer himself to become entangled in money or business affairs. "No man, being a soldier to God, entangleth himself with secular business; that he may please him to whom he hath engaged himself" (II Tim. 2:4). He must be prepared to pitch his

tent anywhere and partake of poor meals. Countless are his
marches and night vigils, his endurance of heat and cold,
wounds from encounters with the enemy, the worst and
greatest of danger, and perhaps in the end death itself—but
a death that is glorious, honorable, and kingly in reward.
During war his life is full of toil and trouble; during peace,
full of glory. He is called the friend of the king; he stands
at his right hand; he may shake hands with his king. Well
then, Christian soldier, learn to know the value of eternal
goods from such trivial earthly examples. Follow your
heavenly King, frustrate the assaults of your invisible foes,
fight bravely against the princes and powers of darkness,
banish them first from your own soul and then from the
souls who have chosen you as their guide and defender. In
all these things you will have to undergo sufferings for
Christ's sake, but precisely because of these sufferings you
will bear off the palm of victory. For you follow Him who
will be victorious in the end and who desires to make you
a partaker in His victory.[146]

We maintain, therefore, that Basil is a true ancestor of
Ignatius. He was transformed by the summons of mystical grace into a "providential" man of the Church.
Both of these men left their solitude to mingle once again
with the world; both, after acting as drill-sergeants for
training "the soldiers of Christ" for centuries to come,
finally wore themselves out in the service of the Church
militant, "in the glory of God." Basil, for whom the
deepest significance of the Christian life lay "in the
glory of God," [147] resembles the Ignatius of Loyola we
have come to know in the final years of his life at Rome.
Hundreds of Basil's letters bear traces of his personality.
He displays a striking social activity. He makes the voice
of Church reform heard in the courts of high politics.

His service of God consists in a loving ministry, that is, in a taking over of "the thousand cares of the Church." [148]

What we have done for St. Basil in these few pages, we should likewise do for St. Benedict; but we shall have to rest content with giving the bare outlines, merely sketching the parallels in the activity and the development of these two great men of the Church.

Ignatius knew and loved St. Benedict. At the Benedictine monasteries of Montserrat and Monte Cassino he spent hours in which he experienced very great graces and the vision on Monte Cassino which he never forgot. [149] He made a very exact study of the Rule of St. Benedict, and some parts of it made their way into the wording of his own Constitutions. [150] In like manner the Rule of St. Benedict contains references which can be traced to St. Ignatius of Antioch [151] and to St. Basil and his Rule. [152] The connection we have traced between Ignatius and Benedict is, then, not wholly arbitrary. Nevertheless, their common mystical call to service in the Church forms an even deeper bond of union between them.

Benedict's task in the history of the world may be summed up in the fact that "he gave a stable order to the strong generation of cenobites." [153] Within the firm hedges of his "enclosure" and his Rule, [154] he boxed in the roving spirit of footloose monks and restricted all merely private and self-centered striving after Christian perfection. One resulting lesson of his Manresa at Subiaco and the first sad monastic experiences of his early youth was that it was impossible to preserve the genuineness of God's spirit and love without a firmly knitted form of obedience. "The fetters of constraint bring the laurels of victory." [155] Hence for Benedict (and in this he shows himself a true Roman with an aristocratic feeling for concise and simple forms in order and discipline), the perfection of obedience was a *schola dominici servitii,* a military school for training soldiers in the service of the king; obedience for him is "a marching towards the royal tabernacle of God." [156] Again, only obedience produces that essential likeness to Christ—"in order that we may by patience share in the sufferings of Christ, and thus merit to be partakers of His Kingdom." [157] Thus the essence of religious life is revealed as a "renouncing of our own will," precisely as in the climax of the Spiritual Exercises at the election, where all perfection is measured by our self-denial. Consequently, the famous sentence in the prologue to Benedict's Rule simply echoes the ideal of the Spiritual Exercises: "To you my words are now directed, you who, having renounced your self-will, have taken up the most powerful and brilliant armor of obedience in order to fight for the Lord Christ, our true King." [158]

Perfection, then, is nothing else than "service of the soldier of God" in the well-established order of the rule.[159] To be perfect, according to St. Benedict, is "to keep oneself in constant readiness for the service of God." [160] Viewed "from below," perfection implies strict obedience, and that is why both Benedict and Ignatius give it a position of paramount importance. But when viewed "from above," perfection means discretion, for it is a superior's discretion, his well-balanced manner of commanding, which imparts a certain nobility to the subject's willingness to obey, which fits all loving willingness to serve into that service proper to the Benedictine monk, singing the praises of God in church.

Again, it was the history-making role of Benedict to have harnessed the vague impulses of the monastic "more" to the "work of God" to which nothing was to be preferred and everything subordinated.[161] As St. Gregory affirms, his Rule is a wise and luminous work.[162] St. Benedict desires that all things be done "with moderation." [163] Hence (and by this discreet mode of action he displays a true stroke of genius), notwithstanding all the limitations he imposes on his ideal of perfection, he can permit every door to stand wide open to God's inspirations, and every possible passage to be cleared that may lead the soul to God [164]—just as St. Ignatius does in his Spiritual Exercises and in his Constitutions. "In his heart he hath disposed to ascend by steps" (Ps. 83:6). The deepest cause for the spiritual kinship between St. Benedict and St. Ignatius, despite the divergence of their historically conditioned and immediate purposes, lies in the mystical sameness of their way of looking at God. Both were men favored with an insight into the abysses of the Godhead and into the effluence of all created things from the hand of the Creator; hence came their prudent sureness in everything related to their lifework, their talent for adapting all things into the scheme of the crucified Christ and His Church and, finally, their discretion and broad outlook. St. Ignatius' vision at Subiaco reminded those in his intimate circle of the vision which St. Benedict had had there.[165] They saw in the account of Benedict's vision, given by St. Gregory the Great, a classical description of what was in Ignatius' own soul the wellspring from which flowed "all his prudence and security in conduct." [166]

The whole world is as nothing to the soul that contemplates the Creator. However little the soul may be illumined by its Creator, in comparison to God the whole world appears insignificant in its eyes. For by the light of interior contemplation the innermost part of the soul is widened and stretches itself towards God in such a way that the soul is lifted up above the world and even above itself. And when the soul feels itself thus exalted, it understands how fleeting is that which passes—a fact which, in its usual lowly condition, it could not understand.[167]

We can and ought to show for St. Augustine, the greatest of all the men of the Church, the working out of the same law in his conversion to the visible and militant Church. We might describe how, shortly after his conversion, he withdrew into the sweet solitude of his Manresas at Cassiacum and Tagaste, into a Platonically proud Christianity of the spirit—a form of Christianity which, according to his own confession, had little or no conception of the humility of the Incarnation and, in consequence, no idea of the Church militant here on earth.[168] Then his second conversion took place, his conversion to the priesthood, to his field of work as a bishop, as head and director of a clerical religious community, and as champion of the poor, miserable, suffering visible Church which wanders like a pilgrim and stranger in this world. During the remainder of his life, he sometimes looked back longingly to that sweet solitude which he had spent alone with God; but it was only to throw himself anew into the battle with even greater vigor.

"Nothing is better, nothing sweeter than to explore the rich treasure of the divine mysteries far from the noise of the world. Such a task is good and agreeable. But to preach, to exhort, to punish, to give edification, to be continually at the beck and call of everyone—that is a great burden, a heavy weight, a crushing labor. Who will not fly from such labors? . . . But the gospel inspires me with terror . . ." [169] Here we have the real Augustine, who, as a man of the Church, also became the model of St. Ignatius. Ignatius studied and applied the Rule of St. Augustine with special care and attention, no doubt because he revered in the works of this great Father of the Church that Augustine who, with his loving discretion, had been changed wholly into the man of the Church.[170] We have already seen what determining influence the theology of St. Augustine exerted upon the origin of the meditation on the Two Standards. Now we see the profound reason why the famous passage on the two kingdoms of Babylon and Jerusalem, and on the two fundamentally motivating forces, love and hatred, which are at work in these two kingdoms, made such a striking impression on the imagination of St. Ignatius.

In Augustine the theology of *The City of God,* written from the depths of his interior soul-life, gave rise to a devoted, but at the same time militant, love of the pilgrim Church, which was constantly at war with the prince of the kingdom of the world. In Ignatius we find the same burning, and yet at the same time, serene joy of battling for the Church under the banner of Christ his Commander-in-Chief, a joy which we can explain only by a grace-imparted insight into the mysteries of God and the

Church given to him at Manresa. Augustine and Ignatius
found their God, not in the blissful solitude of a merely
subjective interior life, but on the battlefield of "a thousand cares for the Church"; and this "solicitude for all
the churches" (II Cor. 11:28) was the criterion by
which they judged the genuineness of the various spirits.

C. CATHERINE AND
BERNARDINE OF SIENA

By way of conclusion to this brief survey on the ancestry of the Ignatian spirit, let us take a swift glance at the
condition of the Church immediately antecedent to
the coming of Ignatius. The age had a false idea about
the nature of the visible Church. For two centuries people lamented over "the five wounds" of the Church.
They saw the Church hopelessly entangled in politics,
commerce and finance, and the fostering of culture and
civilization; they saw it split by schisms and mysteriously
alarmed by prophecies concerning the future Church of
pure spirit. Toward the middle of the fifteenth century
St. Bernardine of Siena complained: "We are surfeited
ad nauseam with prophecies," [171] and he added that the
irreverent curiosity for prying into the mysteries of God
is a satanic outcropping of hatred toward the visible
Church. The consequences flowing from this misguided
flight into mysticism since the fourteenth century, the
aftereffects of the Eckhart exaggerations, the movement
of the "Friends of God" (*Amici Dei*)—all were signs
pointing to the mortal danger the Church had fallen
into, a danger similar to that which had menaced her

very life during the two centuries when Gnosticism had
flourished. Even the stress laid upon simplicity by the
"modern devotion" could not wholly obviate this danger.
In this respect, consider only the anti-Church mysticism
of Wessel Gansfort, with its over-refined "interiority,"
which made so deep an impression upon Martin Luther.[172]
Truth and falsehood were jumbled together; but the
power of discerning between the movements of good and
bad spirits was absent, though the best men of those
times clamored for it.[173] Gerson, the chancellor of the
University of Paris, remarked, "Counterfeit and genuine
coins are being circulated. God's money and the devil's
money are being passed around; and what is most
needed at the present time is, according to our Lord's
word, 'expert money changers.' " [174]

The need of distinguishing between true and false
spiritual coins had already been pointed out by St. Ignatius of Antioch; [175] and in the history of the discernment of spirits the saying "Be ye clever money
changers!" played a very characteristic role from Clem-
ent and Origen down through Jerome to Cassian, where
it became a part of the classical doctrine on the discernment of spirits—after which time it disappeared for
a long while only to turn up once more in the chaotic
conditions of the Reformation period.[176]

An answer to the demand for men capable of discerning spirits is to be found in Ignatius and his Spiritual
Exercises. The earliest Fathers of the Society of Jesus
believed that an efficacious remedy for the evils of that
age was to be found in the "Rules for the Discernment of
Spirits" which stem directly from the substance of the

Exercises, from the meditation on the Two Standards, and are so intimately connected with the "Rules for Thinking Rightly with the Church." In the Directory composed at the direct suggestion of Ignatius, Father A. Gonzales wrote the following words: "Read it in Cassian, who cites a maxim of our Blessed Lord, which, it is true, cannot be found in the Gospels, but which has been quoted by many Fathers of the Church: 'Be ye clever money changers.' And it was precisely for this reason that our Father Ignatius left us these rules." [177]

The two greatest pre-Reformation figures in the ancestry of the Ignatian discernment of spirits were St. Catherine of Siena and St. Bernardine of Siena.

Catherine is a fervent lover of the visible Church with its head at Rome, and the proclaimer of the truth that spirits are proved by their adherence to the Roman papacy. In her *Dialogue* and political letters, we find the same two leading ideas which activated Ignatius at Manresa—namely, a sense for what is from God and what is from the devil in the motions of the innermost soul, and a love that is willing to serve and wear itself out in the service of the hierarchical Church. The internal and the external are indissolubly bound together, because the Church is fighting against Satan and, as a consequence, is capable of "discerning" the innermost motions of the soul by the criterion of love for the Church and by the criterion of vigilant distrust for what is "purely spiritual," extravagant, irreverent and non-human. According to Catherine, the effects of the true spirit are always reverence and humility; these are followed by a sure and prudent joy. "The soul receives a holy fear, and with it a joy and security joined with a sweet prudence that, hesitating, does not hesitate." [178] It is impossible to find a more apt description of the attitude of mind which should be the effect of the Spiritual Exercises and which took flesh, as it were, in Ignatius himself: "sweet prudence." This is the "discreet" love spoken of by the Constitutions. Father Lancicius rightly says that the Society of Jesus venerates in Catherine a model of its own spirit: "Our Society honors Catherine with a very special love, for she was a person who acted throughout her whole life, both in her inner thought and in her outward conduct, in the way that our holy Institute prescribes as a guide." [179]

Bernardine of Siena was the last of the great mystics and men of the Church before the advent of Ignatius. He was penetrated by a world of theological thought that bears close resemblance to the Manresan insight of the relationship between the divine mysteries of our holy Faith. He, too, had envisaged a Kingdom of Christ in the Church militant which fights against Satan, and whose true spirit can be recognized only by the measure of its humble love which serves the visible Church.

Christ, according to Bernardine, is the *Capitaneus Ecclesiae,* the field-captain of a fighting troop.[180] The field on which Satan and Christ meet in battle is the visible Church. So long as the Church plays the part of a pilgrim here below, this battlesite lies "in a plain near Babylon"; and no matter how well-ordered are the files of its army and despite the fact that she is fighting under a King who will ultimately triumph, there is still a possibility of the wily foe's breaking through her ranks.

Jerusalem and Babylon are mixed together. Hence the
need of discernment of spirits. It is precisely in this regard that Bernardine really became a classical forerunner
of the Spiritual Exercises, not so much because he exerted a direct influence upon the writing of the Exercises, but in the much truer sense of a meta-historical
connection between him and the Exercises, insofar as it
is possible to show clearly from his teaching how the
same fruits result from the same mystical insights. We
shall try to illustrate this by a few examples taken from
his "rules for the discernment of spirits." [181]

The first rule reads as follows: "Every motion of the
spirit is to be assented to and accepted if its tendency is
toward hardships and the cross." This is the basic rule
that holds throughout the process of development in all
true asceticism, from the pristine days of the *Didache*
and of the martyr-bishop Ignatius until it finds concise
expression in the third degree of humility in the Spiritual Exercises. The goal which the soul aims at is the
cross, assimilation to the Incarnate God-Man, with an
ardent desire for all that appears to be hardest (nn. 16,
157; cf. MJ II, 1, pp. 779, 816).

This absolutely uncircumscribed "more" of the rules
of St. Bernardine is immediately hedged within its own
proper limits by "discretion." For without this restric-
ing discretion, the "more" immediately sinks to that level
of intemperateness caused by deceiving spirits, which
Bernardine has described so vividly from his own experience. To guard against this danger, therefore, he immediately lays down three further rules, which, in their
astonishing discretion, have a wholly Ignatian ring.

"The motion of the spirit is to be assented to and accepted, provided only that the labors and the cross toward which this motion impels us are capable of being sustained by the human frame." Here Bernardine expresses ideas identical with those voiced by Ignatius in his letter on perfection to the Jesuits residing at Coimbra, even down to the literal wording of Pseudo-Bernard cited by Ignatius.[182] Bernardine's directions are climaxed by the adage of classical antiquity: *Omnibus in rebus est discretio summa*—"In all things discretion is to be ranked first."

The next rule of St. Bernardine is even more basic in its implications. "The motion of the spirit is good and to be approved of if the cross, to which it draws us, is such that the soul is strong enough to bear it." Here the essential love of the cross is set within the bounds of what Ignatius in his later years styled "the measure of grace," and what he repeatedly expressed in the Spiritual Exercises by his discreetly qualifying *dummodo:* "If it should please His Divine Majesty to choose . . ." (nn. 16, 98, 147, 155, 168).

The third rule is perhaps the most remarkable, because it is most truly "Jesuit" in its nature. "The motion of the spirit is to be accepted if the trials and the cross are in accordance with the dictates of sound prudence." Heaven is no further from the earth than is this rule of Bernardine's (and, later, of St. Ignatius and the Spiritual Exercises) from an asceticism and love of the cross based on purely rational naturalism; but we have reverted to that point in the discernment of spirits where an insight into sublime reasonableness was given to Ignatius, a reasonableness which made it possible to go back again to a prudent measure of attention to the world and its affairs, or, in a piquant Ignatian phrase, "to the devotion of ordinary dress." [183]

This supernatural reasonableness has its origin "in illumination of the mind, coming from above, plus the gift of wisdom." But since this light does not diffuse itself necessarily and continuously over unaided reason, upon our natural "manner of knowing," there is a possibility that dangers arising from our fallen nature may threaten our love of the cross thus left to the resources of reason alone. These dangers are impossible to avoid, unless our discernment of spirits is conformed to an objective and unchangeable norm. This norm, however, is obedience to the visible Church. Bernardine, then, lays down for us exactly the same rule for thinking rightly with the Church as that which we find in the Spiritual Exercises: "Every interior joy; every emotion, however exalted; every vision which does not lead us to a faith-inspired love of the divine mysteries preserved in the visible and Roman Church, is to be looked on with suspicion and leads in the end to error, to Satan." [184] That, in short, is what is contained in Bernardine's remaining rules for the discernment of spirits. "O God," he cries out in the passage where he confirms his rules by examples from the experiences of his own life, "how many simple-minded people are duped by the masquerading robes of the evil spirit!" The good spirit urges us to obedience, for the spirit that directs our interior motions is the same as that which directs the Roman Catholic Church. For Bernardine, as later for Ignatius, that law constitutes the most decisive criterion for the discernment of spirits, because it is the most easily observed externally.

Because of the deep knowledge of these things which he had acquired, Bernardine became the Paul-like champion of the Roman Church in his day,[185] picturing so glowingly "the minions and armies of Satan" in his sermons and using them to fight the battle against the foe. To Bernardine the lowly Church of Jesus appears always as the antithesis of the kingdom of Satan's minions. Hence he dedicates the Church again and again to "the sweet name of Jesus," so that eventually he and his fellow preachers are dubbed "Jesuits"—a name invented out of hatred, but full of honor.[186] This title was, so to speak, a prophetic foreshadowing of the company which, a hundred years later, called itself the "Company of Jesus" because "its members believed that they had no other head than Jesus Christ, whom alone they desired to serve." [187] But this service, since the days of Manresa, is service in the hierarchical Church; for the spirit drives on to obedience, mysticism impels to loyalty toward the Holy See, the inner spirit of this ever-growing tendency of "the will to serve" gets its bearings and proportions from the Vicar of Christ. The conclusion of the original text of the vow taken at Montmartre at the very beginning of the Society's existence, is worded as follows: "They vowed to place themselves at the disposal of the Vicar of Christ, in order that he might send them wherever he thought that the interests of God would be best served." [188] On the eve of the founding of the Company, Christ, bearing His cross, together with the Eternal Father, appeared to Ignatius and said to him, "I will

that thou shouldst serve Us." But service to the Blessed
Trinity meant service to Rome. Hence Christ said to
Ignatius, "I will be propitious to you at Rome." [189]

By this Trinitarian love of the papacy, so to speak, by
the whole theological trend of his doctrine on service in
the Church, by his binding together the discernment of
spirits with the objective norm of the visible, militant
Church, Ignatius and his book of Exercises were the prin-
cipal instruments for ushering in, and securing the salvation of, the modern age. It is in this respect that the piety
Ignatius inculcates differs essentially from the "modern
devotion." That is why he felt an almost instinctive
aversion for the literary trivialities of Erasmus, whose
Handbook of a Christian Soldier had the effect of leav-
ing him strangely cool in his religious dealings with
God.[190] Ignatius and Erasmus, two soldiers of Christ,
were worlds asunder, just as Ignatius, the future re-
former, was separated by a whole world from Savonarola, whose *Triumph of the Cross* he praised yet rejected
because he judged Savonarola's spiritual revolt according to the norm of obedience to the hierarchical Church.
"Although Savonarola said many fine things, yet it
seemed to Ignatius that his spirit was not wholly deserv-
ing of approbation; for his spirit was the spirit of rebellion against the Holy See." [191]

Here we will conclude the mystical history of this attitude toward the Church from the Ignatius of the primitive age of the Church down to the Ignatius of modern
times. In tracing this history, we have at the same time
exposed one of those mysteriously occult wellsprings
which supply the Church with entirely new forces pre-

cisely at the moment when she appears to be on the brink
of dissolution—one of those astounding phenomena of
history, comparable only to the sudden inrush of grace
into the soul of a mystic, violently changing the whole
man. The life of the Church is conditioned by the grace
imparted to her great men who have received the Spirit
of God; under the influence of the Spirit, these men
measure the genuineness of their mystical favors by the
humility of the Incarnation and by their willingness and
readiness to obey in all things the bride of Christ, "that
true spouse of Jesus Christ, our holy Mother, the hierarchical Church" (no. 353). This has been the im-
mutable law of change since the first Pentecost, "when
the spirit of God was poured out upon all flesh" (Acts
2:17). Interior and exterior become one. Spirit and
cross, mysticism and obedience, pneuma and Jesus of
Nazareth are henceforward inseparably welded together.
The man of the Church is firmly "convinced that in
Christ our Lord, the Bridegroom, and in His Spouse the
Church, only one Spirit holds sway, which governs and
rules for the salvation of souls" (no. 365). These words
on the last page of the Spiritual Exercises are an epitome
of all that was imparted to Inigo in the mystical illumination at Manresa. Now he is on his way, gathering his
companions and journeying to Rome. When he intro-
duces his Company to the Church, in the presence of the
Holy Father, he crams into his first sentence all that he
has learned from Manresa, from the meditation of the
Two Standards, and from the discernment of spirits.
"This our Society, which we would like to be known by
the name of Jesus, wishes to fight under the banner of

the cross and thus serve God our only Lord, and for the
pope of Rome, His Vicar here on earth." [192]

3. Conclusions

From this study of the origin of the Spiritual Exercises in the mystical depths of Manresa and from our in-
sertion of the Exercises themselves into their proper place
in the history of Christian piety, we are able to fashion a
more deeply penetrating knowledge concerning the ideal
of perfection both as held out to us by the Exercises and
as embodied in the Constitutions of the Society of Jesus.

A. THE SPIRITUAL EXERCISES

First, as to the ideal of perfection found in the Spiritual
Exercises. All that we have said so far is summed up by
Polanco in his preface to the Latin translation of the
Spiritual Exercises, later incorporated into the official
Directory of 1599: "Ignatius wrote the Spiritual Exer-
cises, not so much as a man trained by book-learning,
but as one instructed by the unction of the Holy Spirit,
by the experiences of his interior life, and by practice
gained in the art of directing souls." [193] The innermost
nature of this divine unction is revealed to us by St.
Ignatius, who received a knowledge of the truths of the
Faith such as seemed to epitomize all that is written in
Holy Writ: "These visions strengthened him greatly at
the time and produced such a firmness of faith in him
that ever after he often thought to himself, 'If he had no
knowledge of these mysteries of our holy religion from

the Scriptures, he would still be ready and resolved to die for them, for no other reason than that he had beheld them in these visions.' " [194] He was given an insight into the relationships among all the divine mysteries. This insight he calls faith and knowledge, and contrasts it with all the theological knowledge which he acquired in later life.[195] We can therefore say that throughout his life Ignatius found both in the Scriptures and in theology proper a confirmation of what he had learned at Manresa by the divine unction of the Spirit.

But the obverse of this is also true, that Ignatius, as a man of the Church, remained faithful to the basic law of the discernment of spirits glimpsed at Manresa, in subjecting the substance of his book of Exercises to the dogmatic control of his painfully acquired knowledge of theology, by writing and refining the Exercises over a long period of years. His most personal spiritual goods must prove their genuineness by conforming to the teachings of the hierarchical Church and to the dogmatic teaching of the scholastics, who, he says, were men "instructed and enlightened by the grace of God" (no. 363). Therefore, we easily discern in the Spiritual Exercises evident traces of recasting according to a theological point of view obtained in later years in Paris, Venice and Rome.

Father Nadal testifies to this same fact in words that, besides laying stress on the spiritual unction and Manresan spirit of "God alone," can be understood only of an Ignatius who was not only a mystic, but from the beginning a mystic of the Church: "Before having his book of the Spiritual Exercises printed, Ignatius con-

sulted other books also and took counsel from the length
and breadth of theology. Thus all books, all theologians,
and all Scripture corroborated everything that had been
taught by divine inspiration at Manresa." [196]

Hence, the bull of Pope Paul III, *Pastoralis Officii,*
issued in 1548, formally approving the book of the Spiritual Exercises, could make the statement that the whole
content of this book was drawn "from Holy Writ and
from his experiences in the spiritual life." [197] Dr. Bartolomeo Torres, a most able defender of the Spiritual
Exercises, observed in 1544 that St. Ignatius "speaks the
same language as the philosophers, the saints, and the
Scriptures"; [198] that the content of the Spiritual Exercises is as old as Christianity itself.[199]

Only from a combination of the unction of spirit and
tradition is it possible to gain a complete understanding
of the Spiritual Exercises.

We may quote St. Ignatius. "The Spiritual Exercises
are the most important spiritual weapon in the armory
of the spiritual life, and every retreat master should
make himself an expert in the dexterous use of them." [200]
This dexterity can be achieved in two ways, by *unctio*
and *traditio,* that is, the grace of personal experience and
the study of retreat technique; or, to continue quoting
from the Saint, one must have made the Exercises in
such a way as to experience their full effect (*postquam
expertus fuerit*), and one must be able to give a full account of them (*reddere rationem*). Spiritual experience
and study are the springs which feed one's skill in giving
the Exercises. If with this purpose in view, we refurbish
some ideas taken from the primary sources, our intention

is not to present a colorful chapter from the history of Christian piety, but to give something which is of immediate value at the present day for developing and deepening the interior spiritual life. How necessary this is at a time when the finest treasures of the Christian spirit are indiscriminately massed together! It is because the Exercises, going beyond their own limits and those of the Society, have become a tool so often handled carelessly in the pastoral ministry, that it has become the duty of everyone who aspires to give retreats to make himself an expert in the art of giving the Exercises.

The earliest directories insist again and again on the fact that the Exercises are *to be made;* that, consequently, they are not a book to while away an idle hour, and should not fall into the hands of those who will give them but a cursory reading, culling from them such items only as appeal to their personal spiritual taste.[201] This point is emphasized by Bartolomeo Torres in his defense of the Exercises: "Only he who has passed through this profound and sweet experience will be able to understand fully the meaning of the Spiritual Exercises and at the same time come to recognize the harmony existing between its teaching and that of the Gospels and the Fathers of the Church."[202] He does not even scruple to say that a few days spent in making the Exercises will teach one more real theology than thirty years of reading and studying scholastic theology.[203] We read in the Directory composed by an anonymous Jesuit:

The Exercises do not reveal their secrets except to one experiencing the meditations, just as the Scriptures do not

disclose their profound meaning except to men of deep, interior spirituality. The texts of Holy Writ do not impress us
at a first, casual reading; but if we meditate and ponder
upon them, they are full of mysteries. This holds true also
with regard to the Spiritual Exercises. If we give them a
merely cursory reading, they appear to be a catalogue of
pious, moral instructions and do not make a very strong
impression upon us; but when we really *make* them, they
exercise a tremendous power and influence upon the internal conversion of our souls and their growth in the spiritual life. Experience abundantly testifies to this fact.[204]

For the most part, the penetrating illumination in the
soul of Ignatius, in which the Spiritual Exercises were
born, is not always at our disposal, however much we
ought to pray for this grace. Indeed, what is more needed
for the dark days through which the Church is now passing than daring men who have been enlightened by
mystical graces in their own spiritual experiences, just as
were the men of the Church in the days of Gnosticism
and the Reformation? The first Fathers of the Society of
Jesus were firmly convinced that the tremendous gifts of
prayer vouchsafed to their Father at Manresa were
destined to be passed on as a heritage to his sons.[205] For
the most part, however, only the second way which Ignatius described is open to us—"to make use of books
and allow ourselves to be instructed by theology in its
whole length and breadth." These words can mean only
one thing: that our knowledge of the Spiritual Exercises
and the certainty of our own spiritual experience are to
be enriched by theology. This again is to be effected in
two ways—by our knowledge of the Scriptures and by

secular learning. Concerning this matter the Granada
Directory makes the following remarks:

Whoever desires to give the Exercises to others should
first be fully imbued with the unction of the Holy Spirit;
that is to say, the Holy Ghost is to be the primary instruc-
tor, for both the giver and the maker of the Exercises. The
one who gives the Exercises must be able to discriminate
between the motions of the various spirits, be able to apply
the discernment of spirits (that is, have long experience in
meditating on the Spiritual Exercises), and possess a special skill in the spiritual guidance of souls. Whoever is not
endowed with these gifts must, at the minimum, make a
thorough study of the Exercises and then pray from the
bottom of his heart that God may deign to supply what is
lacking to him.[206]

We must strive to make up by intensive study of the
text of the Exercises what we lack of that gift which St.
Ignatius had by reason of his close union with God, for
seeing directly the connection between all the mysteries
of our holy religion. This study applies, above all, to the
Scriptural testimonies regarding the history of sin, the
Kingdom of Christ and the other mysteries in the life of
our Saviour. Gonzales' Directory makes a point of this
in commenting on the Third Week:

These meditations should be enriched by texts from Holy
Writ—for example, from the Psalms or Isaias, where the
latter speaks about the Passion; above all, by the accounts
of the Passion in the four Gospels. For these words of Holy
Scripture reveal to us the heart of Jesus, act like signposts
on a bright, sunlit day, allowing us to enter into a communion of hearts with Christ crucified, so that we can say
in very truth: "My love is crucified." [207]

An intensive study of theology must compensate for
our deficiency of Ignatius' gift of sudden insight "into
the connection between the mysteries of our Faith and of
the Church." [208] Only in this way can we come to a full
understanding of the Spiritual Exercises. St. Ignatius
demonstrates the bearing of theology on the Spiritual
Exercises in those places where he has made theological
emendations in his original Manresan text. We single out
for comment three main topics.

The first will be the treatment of his theology of sin.
This theology, as found in the original text, was consciously reformulated by Ignatius according to the doctrine of St. Augustine and St. Thomas (no. 50).[209] It is
of the highest importance for the full understanding of
these meditations on sin to think out to their last theological conclusions the relations existing between the
crucified Incarnate Word, the sin of the angels, the fall
of our first parents, sin in general, the sin of the world
(nn. 53, 71). Only thus will it become apparent why
the decision of the battle against Satan is dependent
upon love of the cross, and why love, in the final contemplation to obtain Divine Love, feels itself constrained
to break forth in the *Suscipe:* "Take, O Lord, and receive all my liberty . . ."

From this follows our second main topic, the theology
of the Kingdom of Christ as a war waged against Satan.
In the definitive verbal formulation of the meditation on
the Two Standards, Ignatius, without doubt, had consulted the results of the theological investigations of his
own time. The *abrenuntiatio* of primitive Christianity,
the "renunciation" of Satan and all his pomps [210] which

appeared in Augustine's history of theology, is nothing more than a development of the "renunciation of all things" which we find in the Gospel of St. Luke (14:33) and which there has the meaning of "carrying one's cross" (14:27). This renunciation is extended down through the ages to the basic rule of the Exercises concerning "the surrender of self-love and one's own will and interests" (no. 189). Here a retreat master could weave in the patristic theology on baptism (renunciation of Satan) and its effects upon the ascetical theology of monasticism (renunciation of the world); he could also work in a deepened theology of the life of Christ in order to obviate the possible danger of the dramatic battle of the God-Man's deeds and sufferings losing itself in a series of meditations. Ignatius and the earliest Fathers of the Society of Jesus always strongly emphasized that the meditation on the Kingdom of Christ should act as a quasi-foundation for the Spiritual Exercises,[211] and that the pivotal meditations which decide the others should never change their position in the total structure of the Exercises. Such meditations are, for instance, the visit of Christ to the Temple (nn. 134, 272), and His departure from Nazareth (nn. 158, 159, 163, 273). We shall know how to use all these correctly only if we constantly bear in mind that the Spiritual Exercises are a weapon, an instrument of war, that the real issue in the life of Christ was to expel Satan from this world by means of His own elevation on the cross. "To this end the Son of God appeared, that he might destroy the works of the devil" (I John 3:8).

This leads us on to our third topic, the theology of the

"discernment of spirits." Nowhere is it more evident that Ignatius incorporated into the body of the Spiritual Exercises the results of his post-Manresan study of theology than in the rules for the discernment of spirits and the rules for thinking rightly with the Church, which are closely connected with them.[212] The beginning of Loyola's spiritual experiences and the ultimate total result of his theological study bear the relation to each other of beginning and end. In these rules the grace of personal experience (*unctio*) and technique (*traditio*) have so coalesced as to become inseparable. For this reason, we are all the more justified and obliged to think out to its last details his doctrine on the discernment of spirits and to corroborate it by the superabundant tradition of the Church. In Ignatius' spiritual teaching nothing plays such a decisive role as "consolation and desolation"; again and again he states this in the directories he composed and dictated.[213] It will be impossible to understand and especially to guide the election, the masterpiece of the Spiritual Exercises, without deep theological study. That is why the great spiritual writers of the Society of Jesus—such men as Suarez,[214] Alvarez de Paz,[215] and Scaramelli,[216] to name only a few—treated this theme with a special predilection and appealed again and again to patristic and scholastic tradition in behalf of these rules of St. Ignatius.

B. THE SOCIETY OF JESUS

Thus this praying and deep experiencing of the Spiritual Exercises becomes a re-enactment of those mystical

graces which at one time were produced in the soul of
Inigo. This brings us to the final question that may be
put in an historical account of an ideal of Christian perfection. Is not the drawing up of a groundplan for a new
Order in the Church—which, to be sure, is most intimately connected with the essence of the Spiritual Exercises—a fruit of the mystical hours at Manresa? And
is there a possibility, perhaps, of discovering those mysterious sources in which the universally recognized power
of this Order has its deepest roots?

We are here concerned with that much-discussed question of whether St. Ignatius glimpsed in his vision on
the river Cardoner the essential outlines of the future
Company of Jesus.[217] This is by no means an idle question. Its answer makes us see more clearly how the plan
of the Society arose from the Exercises in the mind of
Ignatius enlightened by grace. It provides at the same
time the true prototype of the Society's nature and ideals.

In the first place, it is an unquestioned historical fact
that Ignatius was wholly in the dark as to the course his
future life was to take. Upon his return from the joyously
penitential pilgrimage to Jerusalem, he asked himself in
all seriousness, "What am I to do now?" [218] He harbored
the thought of entering a decadent order with the object
of there satisfying his burning thirst for humiliation with
Christ.[219] Even between the years 1536–1539, he was
still in doubt as to what form his life was to assume.[220]
His mind was made up about one thing only—"to aid
souls." [221] From the mystical days of Manresa onward,
nothing could shake this idea; it decided every plan for
the future development of his life. Yet together with the

illuminating never-to-be-forgotten grace received on the river Cardoner, we find a darkening ignorance concerning how, concretely, this grace was to be carried into execution and how it would finally lead him to his goal by slow, groping, and halting steps over a period of fifteen long years. "At that time," (after Manresa) says Ribadeneira, "St. Ignatius was still ignorant about the designs of God in his regard. But God knew and directed his steps in such a way as to make him the founder of the Society of Jesus." [222] Nadal gives an even clearer solution of this perplexing riddle concerning the obscure way in which Ignatius was guided: "Imperceptibly and gently Ignatius was drawn toward a goal of which he was still unaware. As yet he had no thought of founding a new Order, and still he strode forward manfully on his way. He pursued his journey with a wise foolishness (*sapienter imprudens*) in the simplicity of a heart that reposed in Christ." [223]

Now, these facts stand in contradiction to equally clear testimony gleaned from the primary sources. From this testimony we learn that, in the composition of his Constitutions even down to such questions as to whether choir was to be retained, whether the novices were to make a pilgrimage, and whether a distinctive habit was to be adopted for the members of his Society, Ignatius appealed time and again with unshakable judgment to that insight given him in the vision on the Cardoner, as though there and then he had been shown the structure of the new Society and even the detailed plans for building it. In confirmation of this we possess six entirely different depositions from two of Ignatius' closest friends, one from Father Gonzales de Camara and five from Father Nadal.

In his *Memoriale,* a journal composed during the months in which he wrote down in closest cooperation with Ignatius the reminiscences of the life of his holy Father, Gonzales notes that Ignatius, when asked for the reasons for giving up a distinctive dress or the choir, at first alleged material reasons drawn from his own practical experience, but then added, "All these questions must be answered by an experience (*negocio*) which I had at Manresa." To these laconic words Father Gonzales, in the final copy of his *Memoriale* which he prepared later in 1573, appends the following explanatory note: "This 'experience' consisted in an extraordinary illumination of his mind in which our Lord revealed these and many other innovations which he has introduced into the Society." [224]

Nadal reports that "For the changes introduced into the Constitutions, as well as for the whole manner of the founding of his Order, St. Ignatius appealed in justification to that sublime illumination of soul which God in His singular goodness granted to him as a great privilege at Manresa in the very beginning of his conversion." [225] In his *Miscellany* written in Spanish—a document from which Astrain took excerpts—Nadal has the following remark: "This is a reference to the vision on the bank of the river Cardoner near the chapel of St. Paul. In that vision he was so rapt above himself that the fundamental laws of all things were manifested to him. During this elevation of spirit it seems that the essential details concerning the institution of the Society were also imparted to him; for, when asked in later years why he arranged this or that matter in this way and not in a different way, his usual reply was: 'For this I appeal to Manresa.' And he often added that this grace surpassed all the other graces put together which he had received throughout his long life." [226]

Father Leturia gives us an extract from an unpublished document of Nadal in which he says:

Ignatius esteemed very highly all through his life this favor which he had received on the river Cardoner. He could not speak of it without experiencing an overwhelming emotion of modesty and humility. Since that day a joyous spiritual light radiated from his countenance. He was accustomed to appeal to this wonderful illumination whenever he was consulted on difficult questions, whenever there was question of something essential for the development of his Order—just as if he had already at that time beheld the meaning and the reasons for all things. [227]

In another manuscript, published for the first time by Father Leturia, Nadal tells us: "Ignatius enjoyed the great privilege of receiving quite early in his spiritual life an enlightenment by the inner guidance of which the Society of Jesus has been brought to its present state." [228]

Father Sacchini has preserved for us an utterance of Father Nadal which expresses the same idea: "Whenever St. Ignatius was asked the reasons for various points in his Constitutions, he was wont to assign, as the last and final ground for his action, that sublime illumination at Manresa conferred upon him by God in His great goodness and condescension; it is as though he had received from God at that time the spirit and wisdom of a master

builder" (*quasi in spiritu quodam sapientiae architec-
tonico*).[229]

These clear evidences show beyond doubt that St. Ignatius appealed for the basic characteristics and details
of his Constitutions to the mystical grace received on the
river Cardoner. Against the exaggerations of Father J.
Creixell and other Spanish commentators, Fathers Van
Ortroy and Leturia have demonstrated how this firmness
of mind can be reconciled with the equally firmly established fact of his uncertainty, lasting over a long period
of years, in regard to his future vocation and with his
long labor in working out the Constitutions and inten-
sively studying the Rules of other Orders. At Manresa
Ignatius saw only the barest outlines of his Company,
from which it was later possible to derive its nature and
tasks; but he saw them so penetratingly and luminously
that it seemed to him in later years that everything he
planned to accomplish through his Society fitted in
exactly with the basic scheme which had flashed upon
him in his vision on the river Cardoner. With the "wisdom of a master builder" he saw there the outlines of a
life-achievement that advanced, in strict logical sequence,
from a desire "to help souls" to the foundation of the
Society. For this Father Orlandini has coined the apt
expression: "At Manresa Ignatius saw the *fabrica
Societatis,* the blueprints of the Society of Jesus." [230]

This solution can be given greater depth by keeping in
mind the peculiar blend of darkness and light characteristic of every mystical experience. What the intellect,
left to its own natural resources, must seek over a long
period of years in the field of knowledge and acquire

laboriously from experience, study and tradition, now becomes a confirmation of what the mind, raised above itself, sees in one instantaneous, lightninglike glance. It is plain that there is no incompatibility at all between the dark uncertainty that follows upon a mystical experience and the clear certainty in which all knowledge is considered as the result of one mystical grace.[231]

We may advance one step further in our explanation of the mystical origin of the Society of Jesus. For this step, too, we possess trustworthy primary sources. In the vision granted him at Cardoner St. Ignatius saw in one view all the mysteries of God and the Church, and also the outlines of his future Society. This is undoubtedly the same world of thought from which he fashioned, while still at Manresa, the meditation on the Two Standards. Father Luis de la Palma speaks of an oral tradition about St. Ignatius (a quite secondhand tradition): "I have heard Father Aegidius Gonzales say that he was present when Father Everard Mercurian, the fourth General of the Society, delivered an instruction in which he said that he had it from the lips of our holy Father Ignatius himself that God had shown him the plan and the outlines of the Society in the meditation on the Two Standards." [232] On the basis of the same oral tradition Father Lancicius gives the following account: "While Ignatius of Loyola, in the very first stages of his conversion, was writing out the Spiritual Exercises, God disclosed to him in the meditation on the Two Standards the whole form of the Society he was to found, the whole structure of this marvelous edifice." [233]

We do not find this tradition, at least not in this precise form, in the printed copies of the instructions of

Father Everard Mercurian.[234] Though this is true, it is
no justification for Father Von Ortroy's skepticism regarding the tradition, for Father Mercurian could have
omitted these more intimate details when he had his instructions printed. At any rate, it was the oldest tradition
among those who had known Ignatius personally that
the meditation on the Two Standards, with its petition
to be received under the banner of the poor Jesus, was
the birth-hour of the Society of Jesus. A distinct proof of
this assertion is seen in the fact that Ignatius regarded
the vision of La Storta [235] as the fulfillment of the colloquy in the meditation on the Two Standards (no.
147): namely, as proof that he was now definitely and
finally received under the banner of Christ. We have a
verification of the same fact in the mystical perception
he noted down on February 23, 1544: "I recalled to
mind that moment when the Heavenly Father associated
me with His Divine Son, and I felt a burning longing
that He might engrave deeply within my heart the name
of Jesus." [236] Now the journey is over. Of the whole pilgrimage from the vision near the chapel of St. Paul to
the basilica of St. Paul at Rome, it remains true: "Imperceptibly and gently Ignatius was being conducted
toward a goal of which he himself was still unaware—but
with the wisdom of a master builder."

C. OTHER CONCLUSIONS

From what we have just said, a few final and grave
conclusions may be drawn that will lead us to a deeper
understanding of the ideal of perfection which the Society
of Jesus professes within the limits of the Church.

The first consequence is that in the origin of the Spiritual Exercises from the Manresan mysticism, as delineated above, with its clear basic lines and its humble quest for the way, continued over the years with eyes open to all possibilities, we have a classic example of what we came to know when we spoke of the theology of the "more" in the opening pages of this book. There is one thing and one thing only that St. Ignatius desires—to aid Christ his King by the saving of souls. All else is subject to change and is left to the gradual revelations of the promptings of grace; all else goes from what is high to what is higher and is essentially limitless, except it be the inexorable clarity of the purpose of the will to serve souls in the Church militant here on earth. This is the complement of what we perceived in the beginning of this book as the Ignatian "of and at" (see page 6 of the text); now its meaning is: Ignatius departs from Manresa and arrives at the inexhaustible fullness of the possibilities toward which he is spurred by the "more" of his zeal for souls. He remains still a *caballero de Dios,* a "noble knight of God" setting out as the founder of an Order to conquer new lands for his King.

He bequeathed this ideal to his Order. The innermost purpose of his Society ever consists in helping souls, *ayudar las animas,* and everything else in it is, without exception, subordinated to this end. Suarez treats this point masterfully in his tractate *De Religione Societatis.* "Personal sanctification, prayer, penance, external conduct—all is to be subordinated to, and determined by, the purpose of aiding souls. The Society of Jesus seeks the perfection of its members in such a way that it desires that complete perfection, and all the means of attaining it, to minister to the perfection of the neighbor." [237] Consequently all the gates of the driving "more" lie wide open to these systematic functions of service; Ignatius has left them wide open, both in the Spiritual Exercises and in the Constitutions, as paths of ascent to God and as ways to an ever-increasing union with God sufficiently marked off by the ideal of helping souls and clearly defined by his meditation on the Two Standards and by the Constitutions as a whole. Just as Ignatius could find justification throughout his life for even the apparently smallest details by the words "I appeal to Manresa for this," so, from that time on, every noble-minded soldier of the Company shares in the privilege of his Father St. Ignatius of making constant appeal throughout his life to the slogan: *I appeal to the Constitutions;* that is, I enclose the immoderate urging of my "more" within the hedge of obedience. "For this is the mark by which the true sons of the Society are known." [238] In obedience, consequently, the same law of life holds for every Jesuit that was operative in St. Ignatius. Because of it, "he was led gently whither he knew not—but in the spirit and wisdom of a master builder." The obedient soldier is wisely imprudent.

The second consequence is this: because the Society of Jesus sprang from the fundamental meditation on the Two Standards, its helping souls takes the form of a battle for Christ, who still lives in His Kingdom, which is struggling on earth. The first meaning of "Church militant" certainly is not the mere outward conflict of its mission in history, and consequently not what may be called the apologetical aspect of its life. The term in the Spiritual Exercises (no. 352) signifies, according to the formulation of E. Przywara, "not the Church militant in the sense of a definite combat or an attitude of conflict, but the Church in discipline and obedience rendering service. Therefore no mention is ever made in the rules of a particular struggle or of a military attitude toward any opponent, but only of the attitude of the members of the Church toward the proper ecclesiastical authorities or that of the members toward one another." [239] Just as in the meditation on the Kingdom of Christ, the unbounded enthusiasm of the soldier and knight has a surprisingly sober outcome, resulting not in "the conquest of the whole world" but in a petition to imitate Christ in poverty and abuse (no. 98), so in the meditation on the Two Standards we ask to be received under the banner of Christ and, without more ado, beg for a love of shame and contempt (no. 147). This parallel means that the net result of the enthusiasm engendered by these two meditations has a common goal in the conclusion of the election which strikes through the center of the human heart: "to divest oneself of all self-love, self-will, and self-seeking" (no. 189).

The pivot on which everything turns, therefore, is not some plan for the conquest of an enemy from without—in the sense, for example, of a crusade which may be all too lightly conceived—but rather a campaign that strikes into our very hearts in order to overthrow the enemy of our human nature in this sector of the front. But all of this must be accomplished by a grace-given insight that precisely in this way the soul may become a delicately fashioned instrument which God can use for the help of souls and the reconquest of the Kingdom of Christ. "What wonder that when our own hearts are first changed by the grace of God we are able to effect a change in the world outside ourselves by our own activity?" [240] This sentence conceals the most profound theology of Church history, as well as the theology of that spirit which won all the victories that the Society of Jesus has been able to inscribe on its banner during the course of the last four centuries; it gives insight into the Society's deepest secret, that from which the goodness or dubiousness of its triumphs may be judged. Its battle can be a battle only in the sense of the Two Standards, and hence, above all else, a battle against self, for it "fights under the banner of the cross." That is the true conclusion toward which Ignatius directs all the enthusiasm and love of his soldiers in the Spiritual Exercises.

Precisely because of the pivotal position which this "care of souls" occupies in the Spiritual Exercises, it is frequently necessary to call attention to its meaning and the manner in which it is to be carried out in the Church. It is not a mere apostolate, falsely understood and showing itself in merely external activity; nor is it a worldly ideal, rejoicing in well-organized, statistically provable results; rather, it is the discipline of an obedient soldier, ever on the alert, ever ready to spring into action and to make numberless sacrifices, never counting the cost, yet in the end, when he has done all in his power, ready to confess that he is "a useless servant, stripping himself of all his self-will."

All of this is tantamount to saying that our ideal must never falter, never doubt the final triumph of the visible Church, never retreat from the front-line, or show contempt for visible results achieved by the Church, a contempt that in the final analysis has its roots in pride. For

just as the battle against our own flesh and blood turns
out, so also will the battle for the Kingdom of the Incarnate Word, made visible in flesh and blood, and the
battle in His Church militant. The Jesuit is not a Gnostic
or a Monophysite in matters relating to the Church,
because he fights, to quote Ignatius of Antioch, "for Him
who was really born and ate and drank, really perse-
cuted under Pontius Pilate, really crucified and really
rose from the dead." [241] The type of self-denial peculiar
to Jesuit spirituality (entailing the sacrifice of a strict
manner of living, a definitely fixed dress and method of
practising penance, in order to live a life comparable to
that of secular priests) [242] does not keep the Jesuit from,
but rather binds him more to, that continual mortifica-
tion demanded by a stern struggle against self in the
visible and "ordinary" Church.

A still further consequence stems from the nature of
St. Ignatius' Order and the nature of his ideal of spiritual perfection. We here touch a very sensitive nerve
which too often responds painfully to the slightest stimu-
lus—that is, the hatred which the Society of Jesus has
ever encountered and which is repeatedly attested to in
the pages of Church history. It does not surprise us that
the enemies of Christ should hate the Society. This lot it
has in common with every other religious Order, with
the Church itself, and her crucified Master. We can
make a worthwhile attempt to arrive at a deepened theological basis for this silent, often almost instinctive, aversion that the Society of Jesus encounters, even within the
pale of the Church. Persecution, it may be said, is almost
a part of the Society's inheritance from the first days of
its existence. The Jesuit theologian Suarez, [243] by ex-

plaining the nature of the ideal of perfection that the Society of Jesus wishes to represent, made the first attempt to lay bare the causes for this hostile attitude. He investigates the strange feelings of aversion that animated the ecclesiastical circles of his day—feelings expressed in accusations of arrogance, craze for novel methods, and rejection of tradition. Many human failings may have afforded justifiable grounds for this adverse attitude; but basically it had its cause in the nature which Ignatius communicated to his Order, in its "illimitability" (to be measured only by Christ and the daily battle for salvation in His Church), and in its readiness to dare and do all, never allowing itself to be wholly confined within the limits of peaceful forms and tasks. This spirit gave rise in the Order's opponents to a feeling of being threatened; it was an apprehension which may have gripped ecclesiastical circles because of the Jesuits' ever changing tactics, their unwelcome interference, their constant pushing forward, their Pauline "solicitude for all the churches" which they made their own. Suarez enlarges especially upon the charge that the Society of Jesus because of its very name (which, properly speaking, is more appropriate to the Church as a whole) wished to express how greatly it felt itself obligated to guide the destinies of the universal Church. His answer to this objection is couched in the following words: "The Order did not take the name of 'Society of Jesus' in order arrogantly to claim authority over the universal Church (*ut universalem ecclesiam sibi arrogaret*), but in order to show itself a true and especially obedient daughter of the Church." [244]

We shall insert here those particular elements which

flowed from the mystical origin of the Ignatian ideal of perfection concerning his Order. The Jesuit is called to be an active soldier in the service of the Church under the banner of the cross; this must be the measure by which we gauge the ideals and the dangers of his activity as well as the justice and injustice of the criticism levelled against him. Where his tactics exceed the limits of service under the standard of the cross, they are rightly rejected. But as long as a Jesuit's line of action is in conformity with the deepest purpose of his calling, he is under the obligation of giving himself totally, and of keeping alive, "in season and out of season" (II Tim. 4:2), that life-giving restlessness without which it is impossible for the frontline of Christ his King to advance. The Company is ever in active military service and therefore its tactics are never fixed and rigid, except where they are influenced by the standard of the cross—that is to say, by the example of its crucified Master and by obedience. In this sense, it is true to say of the Society of Jesus "that it is slowly and gently being led toward a goal of which it is still ignorant." Concerning the battle it is fighting, nothing is certain but victory itself; the possible number of battle phases with their changing frontline positions is still hidden from us. Our share in the victory of our royal Master, we know, will be in proportion to our share in His labors and sufferings (no. 93), that is, to speak in concrete terms, our share of Christ's triumph will depend upon our obedience to the hierarchical Church, upon the "wise foolishness of a simple and undivided heart that rests in Christ." So long as this is the only foundation for the enmity displayed toward the Society

of Jesus, so long must it regard and bear this hatred as
an inseparable part of its stern military regime and discipline; since, when we beg to be received under the
standard of the cross, we also beg to be allowed to suffer
poverty, humiliation, and contempt with Christ our
Leader (no. 147). This petition is presented with the
seemingly astonishing condition, "provided only that I
can suffer these without sin on the part of another, and
without offense of His Divine Majesty." For obviously
there are those who, in spite of good will and upright intentions, humiliate and wrong others, but who are, none-
theless, serving the Divine Majesty in the same manner
and standing in the same battle line as those they injure.
It follows, therefore, that as long as our terrestrial battle
front is occupied by men of God, "all slander, insults,
and blind charges of folly" [245] cannot be altogether
erased, but are to be borne patiently for the sake of the
general victory. "But what of it? Provided only that in
every way, whether in pretense or in truth, Christ is being proclaimed; in this I rejoice, yes, and I shall rejoice"
(Phil. 1:18).

Therefore, we may sum up the results of this historical
survey on the ideal of perfection, as it should be lived in
the Spiritual Exercises and in the Society of Jesus, in the
following words: "Service in the Church, under the banner of the cross, for the glory of the Father." During the
early days of the Society of Jesus, Father Nadal proclaimed this ideal to his fellow Jesuits in words deriving
their full power from Ignatius' mysticism at Manresa.
"We must deeply familiarize ourselves with the thought
that we are followers of Jesus Christ, who, even at the

present time, is carrying His Cross in the Church militant. We are to come after Him bearing our own cross; it is for this purpose that the Eternal Father has made us His servants." [246]

The spirit in which such service is to be rendered "for the greater glory of God" is love, a love which manifests itself more in deeds than in words (no. 230), a love that at the greatest height of total immolation permits itself in all holy sobriety to formulate the petition: "Give me thy love and thy grace, for this is sufficient for me" (no. 234). This is the "discreet love" of the nobleman, the manly loyal sense of the soldier of Christ, that was first formed in the soul of Ignatius and is now to be impressed upon those who are forming themselves in the school of perfection: love of discipline, reverence, and self-forgetfulness. It is that love for which Ignatius, again and again, earnestly prays in his mystical journal: "Give me loving humility and loving reverence." [247]

In his directions on how to give the Spiritual Exercises, Ignatius has summed up in one succinct phrase the attitude of soul in which the Spiritual Exercises should be made. The phrase is, as it were, the distilled essence of his whole personality and, consequently, of the ideal of perfection in his Company; it is a ringing challenge to the best souls of our age, souls who feel called to give their whole service to the Church "like noble knights of Christ!" [248]

Como noble caballero de Christo!

Notes

Abbreviations and Notes on Primary Sources

MH = *Monumenta Historica Societatis Jesu,* a collection of all the sources on the origins of the Society of Jesus in seventy-one volumes, published at Madrid and Rome from 1894 to 1948.
  Certain sections of this collection have been used in the present volume:

MH Chron. Pol. = *Chronicon Joannis Alphonsi de Polanco,* a chronological six-volume history of the Society of Jesus. We cite mainly the first volume on the life of Ignatius (*Vita Ignatii Loyolae et rerum Societatis Jesu historia,* Madrid, 1894).

MH Nadal = *Monumenta Patris Hieronymi Nadal,* his letters, instructions, and a journal of his confidential dealings with Ignatius, Madrid, 1898–1905.

MI = *Monumenta Ignatiana.* This is the original text of St. Ignatius' writings. It is divided into four parts, to each of which we append a number:

MI^1 = Twelve volumes of Ignatian letters, Madrid, 1903–1912.

MI^2 = The critical text of the book of the *Spiritual Exercises* and its first commentaries, one volume, Madrid, 1919. We use the translation of the Exercises by Louis J. Puhl, S.J., The Newman Press, Westminster, Maryland, 1951.

MI^3 = The critical Latin and Spanish text of the *Constitutions* of the Society of Jesus, three volumes, Rome, 1934–1938.

113

$MI^4 =$ Two volumes bringing together various memoirs, documents, evaluations of the times, and the acts of the canonization of St. Ignatius. A new edition in three volumes is now in preparation; the first tome was published at Rome in 1944.

$AB =$ The memoirs or so-called "autobiography" of St. Ignatius, which he dictated to Father Louis Gonzales de Camara. The original text can be found in the *Monumenta Ignatiana, I,* which is Volume 66 of the *Monumenta Historica Societatis Jesu,* Rome, 1943. An English rendering was done by J. F. X. O'Conor, S.J., and published as *The Autobiography of St. Ignatius Loyola,* New York, 1900. Although references are made to Father O'Conor's translation, we have not followed his work verbatim.

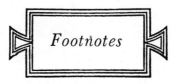

Footnotes

Chapter I

[1] *MH Chron. Pol.,* I, 516, Appendix II, *De S. Ignatii genealogia.*

[2] *MH Chron. Pol.,* II, 267; I, 517. Leturia, *El Gentilhombre,* p. 47. (Owen, *Iñigo de Loyola,* p. 31.)

[3] *MH Nadal,* IV, 825.

[4] *MI⁴,* II, 192 f.; *MH Chron. Pol.,* VI, 44. Leturia, *El Gentilhombre,* pp. 30 f. (Owen, *Iñigo de Loyola,* pp. 18–19.)

[5] Leturia, *Gentilhombre,* p. 33. (Owen, *Iñigo,* p. 20. We have not followed Father Owen's translation, since the order of certain sentences and paragraphs from Father Leturia's work have been altered by Father Rahner for purposes of condensation.)

[6] Huonder, *Ignatius von Loyola,* p. 33.

[7] Leturia, *Gentilhombre,* pp. 35 f. (Owen, *Iñigo,* pp. 20 ff.)

[8] *Dialogi Patris Natalis,* folio 47 v. (*Archivum Romanum Societatis Jesu*); in Leturia, *Gentilhombre,* p. 38. (Owen, *Iñigo,* p. 35.)

[9] *AB,* VI (O'Conor, *The Autobiography of St. Ignatius,* p. 25). Cf. Leturia, *Gentilhombre,* pp. 56 and 149. (Owen, *Iñigo,* pp. 59–60 and 100.) F. de Llanos y Torriglia, "El capitán Inigo de Loyola y la dama de sus pensamientos," in *Razon y Fe,* CXXIV (1941), 33–69.

[10] Leturia, "Notas criticas sobre la Dama del Capitán Loyola," in *Archivum historicum Societatis Jesu,* V (1936), 84–92. (Owen, *Iñigo,* p. 53, 59–60.) The castle was gloomy because of Joanna; actually it was one of the most beautiful in Spain.

[11] Leturia, *Gentilhombre,* p. 57, note 54. (Owen, *Iñigo,* p. 38, note 55.)

[12] Polanco, *Sumario* (*Archivum Romanum Societatis Jesu*) cf. *Fontes Narr.,* I, 154; Leturia, *Gentilhombre,* p. 70 (Owen, *Iñigo,* p. 42–43); Paul Dudon, *St. Ignatius of Loyola,* translated by William J. Young, Milwaukee, 1949, pp. 37–38.

[13] *AB,* I (O'Conor, p. 19).

[14] *MI⁴,* I, 37 and 101.

[14a] These numbers in parentheses which will occur frequently refer to the marginal numbers in *The Spiritual Exercises of St. Ignatius,* translated by Louis J. Puhl.

[15] Compare Erik Przywara, *Crucis Mysterium* (Paderborn, 1939), pp. 202–214, "The Idea of the Jesuit in the Liturgy."

[16] From the so-called "Maxims of Our Holy Father Ignatius," *MI¹,* XII, 679. Cf. H. Rahner, *Ignatius von Loyola, Geistliche Briefe* (Spiritual Letters of St. Ignatius), Einsiedeln, 1942, p. 283.

[17] Huonder, *Ignatius,* p. 99.

[18] *Ibid.,* pp. 298 f.

[19] Text in Tacchi-Venturi, *Storia della Compagnia di Gesu* (Rome, 1922), I, 615.

Chapter II

[20] *AB,* V (O'Conor, p. 24).

[21] Cf. W. Kreiten, "Zur Entstehung des Exerzitienbüchleins

(Origin of the book of the Exercises)," in *Stimmen aus Maria Laach,* XXIII (1882), 39.

[22] *MH Chron. Pol.,* I, 37.

[23] *MH Nadal,* IV, 825 f.

[24] *AB,* XIII (O'Conor, p. 31).

[25] Leturia, *Gentilhombre,* p. 61. (Owen, *Iñigo,* p. 39; cf. also Appendix I.) While Inigo was still a young boy, his sister (his cousin, according to Leturia) entered the convent of San Pedro de Elormendi under Franciscan reform, where she took the name "Isabelita"; Leturia, pp. 28 f. (Owen, *Iñigo,* p. 13, says it was Inigo's aunt.)

[26] *Historia de la Compania de Jesus,* I, 18.

[27] *MH Chron. Pol.,* I, 13.

[28] *AB,* III (O'Conor, p. 22).

[29] *AB,* XII (O'Conor, pp. 27 and 32); Feder, pp. 29 and 125, note 19.

[30] *MI⁴,* I, 726.

[31] *AB,* XV (O'Conor, p. 34).

[32] *AB,* XIV (O'Conor, p. 31).

[33] *MH Chron. Pol.,* I, 14 f.

[34] *MH Chron. Pol.,* I, 13: "Minus utique contra Deum verbum ullum blasphemiae fuit ab ipso umquam auditum, licet aliquando in afflictiones et labores multos incidisset."

[35] *AB,* XII (O'Conor, p. 24).

[36] *MH Chron. Pol.,* I, 13.

[37] *Ibid.,* p. 10: "Erant in illo quaedam naturalia Dei dona non vulgaria; nam in primis animosus valde ad res arduas aggrediendas, et constans ad persequendas et prudens ad easdem dirigendas exstitit."

[38] *MI⁴,* I, 200.

[39] *AB,* XI (O'Conor, p. 29); Dudon-Young, p. 46.

[40] *AB,* VII (O'Conor, p. 25).

[41] Text of *Cod. Instit. Soc. Jesu,* 98, folio, 140 v., first published by Leturia in his article, "El influjo de San Onofre in San Ignacio," *Manresa,* II (1926), 229.

[42] *AB,* VII (O'Conor, p. 25).

[43] There is a facsimile of the text from the Preface to the Spanish *Vita Christi* in Leturia's *Gentilhombre,* p. 137.

[44] *AB,* IX (O'Conor, p. 28).

[45] Text in Leturia, *Gentilhombre,* pp. 160–161.

[46] *Legenda aurea Sanctorum* (Madrid, 1688), p. 435. *Flos Sanctorum,* no. 124 (112), "Vita Augustini," Latin edition by Thomas Graesse, third edition (Breslau, 1890), p. 558. French edition, *La Légende dorée,* translated by Theodore de Wyzewa, Paris, 1935, p. 466. English edition, *The Golden Legend,* translated by Granger Ryan and Helmut Ripperger, 2 Vols., London, 1941—C. A. Kneller was the first to call attention to this text in *Zeitschrift für katholische Theologie,* XLIX (1925), 164, note 5.

[47] *AB,* XI (O'Conor, p. 29).

[48] The text of the *Flos Sanctorum* is taken from St. Augustine's *De Civitate Dei,* vol. XIV, chap. 28 (*PL* 41, 436); also *Enarrationes in Psalmos,* 61, 6, and 64, 2 (*PL* 36, 733–734 and 773).

[49] *AB,* VIII and IX (O'Conor, pp. 26–27).

[50] *MI²,* I (Volume on the *Exercises*), p. 80.

[51] *AB,* XII.

[52] In the introduction to the Spanish edition of the *Flos Sanctorum* the saints are called "*Caballeros de Dios.*" Cf. Leturia, *Gentilhombre,* p. 161.

[53] *AB,* XII and XVI (O'Conor, pp. 27 and 32).

[54] See the Spanish text in Leturia, *Gentilhombre,* p. 156 (Owen,

Iñigo, p. 174.) The Latin original can be found in the life of St. Onuphrius by St. Paphnutius, *Vitae Patrum (PL* 73, 213–222).

⁵⁵ The text of this hymn to St. Francis is contained in "Cancionero" of Fray Ambrosio Montesino, in Leturia, *Gentilhombre,* p. 61. (Owen, *Iñigo,* p. 168–9.)

⁵⁶ *Flos Sanctorum,* pp. 112–3, "Vita Dominici."

⁵⁷ *Flos Sanctorum,* pp. 147–9, "Vita Francisci." English translation, II, 597.

⁵⁸ *AB,* VII (O'Conor, p. 26).

⁵⁹ Oliver Manare, *Exhortationes* (Brussels edition, 1912, p. 344). Cf. A. Codina, *Entstehung der Exerzitien, Studien zu den Exerzitien des hl. Ignatius (Contributions to the History of the Spiritual Exercises),* Vol. I, edited by G. Harasarr, Innsbruck, 1925, p. 39, note 25.

⁶⁰ *AB,* XVII (O'Conor, p. 36).

⁶¹ *Dialogi de Instituto* (as yet not published as a whole; cited by A. Codina, *Entstehung der Exerzitien,* p. 38, note 5): "Hic Manresae Deus illi Exercitia communicavit, qua via illum ita gubernavit, ut se totum Dei gloriae et hominum saluti manciparet. Quam rem Ignatius duobus exercitiis, Regis et Vexillorum, maxime intellexit."

⁶² *AB,* XI (O'Conor, p. 24); Dudon-Young, pp. 43–44.

⁶³ See the *Directoria Antiquissima,* especially the *Directoria ignatiana autographa, MI²,* I, 779–780, 784, 789–790.

⁶⁴ *MI²,* I, 784.

⁶⁵ On this subject compare J. A. Otto, "Werden end Wesen des Ignatianischen Missionwillens" in *Missionswissenschaft und Religionswissenschaft,* III (1940), 112–113. P. Kellerwessel, "Geschichtliches zur Konigsbetrachtung der Exerzitien," in *Zeitschrift für Aszese und Mystik,* VIII (1932), 70–79. W. Sierp, "Einige Gedanken zur Christkönigsbetrachtung der Ignat. Exercitien," in the same review, V (1930), 324–334.

A. Huonder, "Ein Flottenplan des hl. Ignatius," in the *Katholische Missionen,* XLIII (1915), 49–53.

[66] *MI²,* I, 786.

[67] *Constitutiones* I, 2, 6 (*MI³,* III, 49); I, 3, 12, p. 54. Cf. also the letter of Ignatius to Father Le Jay, dated December 15, 1551 (*MI¹,* IV, 37).

[68] *Constitutiones* IX, 2, 6 (p. 246).

[69] *MI⁴,* I, 263.

[70] *Examen Generale* I, 6 (*MI³,* III, 4).

[71] *Constitutiones* III, 1, 25 (p. 91).

[72] Cf. Karl Rahner, "Die Ignatianische Mystik der Weltfreudig-keit," in *Zeitschrift für Aszese und Mystik,* XII (1937), 121–137.

Chapter III

[73] *AB,* XVIII (O'Conor, p. 38).

[74] *AB,* XXI (O'Conor, p. 44).

[75] *AB,* XXVII (O'Conor, p. 52).

[76] *MH Nadal,* IV, 666.

[77] *MH Chron. Pol.,* I, 25.

[78] *MI¹,* I, 105.

[79] *AB,* XXXI (O'Conor, p. 57).

[80] *AB,* XXI (O'Conor, p. 43).

[81] *AB,* XX (O'Conor, p. 41).

[82] *AB,* XIX (O'Conor, pp. 40–41).

[83] *AB,* XXVI (O'Conor, p. 51).

[84] *AB,* XXV (O'Conor, p. 50).

[85] *AB,* XXVIII (O'Conor, p. 53).

[86] *AB,* XXIX (O'Conor, pp. 54–55). Cf. Hugo Rahner, in the *Zeitschrift für Aszese und Mystik,* X (1925), 206 ff. *MH Chron. Pol.,* I, 22: "Miras a Domino illustrationes circa mysterium Sanctissimae Trinitatis et mundi creationem et alia fidei mysteria eo tempore, quo Manresae versatus est, accepit."

[87] *AB,* XXX (O'Conor, p. 57).

[88] *MI*⁴, I, 473.

[89] "Genesis de los Ejercicios," in the *Archivum historicum Societatis Jesu,* X (1941), 26.

[90] *MH Chron. Pol.,* I, 20.

[91] An hitherto unpublished sermon of Father Nadal at Salamanca, 1554, *Archivum historicum Societatis Jesu,* XCVIII, folio 102; Father Leturia has published extracts in his "Genesis de los Ejercicios," pp. 54–55. Cf. also *Monumenta Historica Fontes,* "Narrativi" (Rome, 1943), I, 307–308, for photostatic reproduction.

[92] Leturia, "Genesis de los Ejercicios," p. 26. Cf. J. A. Otto, *Werden und Wesen des Ignatianischen Missionwillens,* pp. 115–117.

[93] *AB,* XXIX (O'Conor, p. 55).

[94] Leturia, "Genesis de los Ejercicios," p. 28.

[95] *AB,* XXXIV (O'Conor, p. 61).

[96] *AB,* XLV (O'Conor, p. 73).

[97] *MI*⁴, I, 104.

[98] *Sumario* of the year 1548 (as yet unpublished); extracts are in Leturia, "Genesis de los Ejercicios," p. 53.

[99] *MH Nadal,* IV, 826.

[100] *MI*¹, I, 106, in a letter to Sister Teresa Rejadella, June 18, 1536.

[101] *The Spiritual Exercises,* no. 365.

[102] *MH*[1], I, 529, a letter to Francis Borgia. Cf. Hugo Rahner, "Woher stammt der Name Ignatius?" in *Mitteilungen* of the German Province, CIV (1936), 13–18.

[103] *MI*[1], XII, 678. These maxims of St. Ignatius, headed by "My love is crucified," have been edited and published in a German translation by Hugo Rahner: *Ignatius von Loyola, Geistliche Briefe (Spiritual Letters)*, Einsiedeln, 1942, pp. 282 ff. St. Ignatius words the statement, "Jesus, my love is crucified." This gives a different sense to the apothegm from that given to it by Ignatius of Antioch, who confessed in his letter to the Romans, VII, 2, "My love is crucified," that is, my love for the world is nailed to the cross (*The Epistles of St. Ignatius of Antioch,* translated by James A. Kleist, The Newman Press, Westminster, 1946, p. 83). St. Ignatius saw this saying for the first time in the *Flos Sanctorum,* life of St. Ignatius of Antioch, given as a citation from Pseudo-Dionysius, *De divinis Nominibus,* IV, 12 (PG 3, 709 B).

[104] *Didache,* XI, 8 (James A. Kleist, *The Didache,* 1948, p. 22).

[105] Pastor Hermas, *Mandatum,* XI, 7–8 (Joseph Marique, "The Shepherd of Hermas," in *The Apostolic Fathers,* New York, 1947).

[106] Cf. Ignatius of Antioch's *To the Smyrnaeans,* V, 2 (Kleist, p. 92). Cf. also *Trallians,* X (Kleist, p. 78).

[107] *To the Ephesians,* V, 2–3 (Kleist, p. 62); *Trallians,* VII, 2 (p. 77); *Smyrnaeans,* VII, 1–2 (p. 92); *Philadelphians,* IV, 1 (p. 85).

[108] *Smyrnaeans,* VI, 2 (p. 92).

[109] *MI*[4], I, 100. This "natural fire" is then transferred into spiritual and mystical regions, from the "generous heart, inflamed by love of God" of his days of conversion (*AB,* IX; O'Conor, p. 28), to the "inner fire" of the mystic ardor (*Spiritual Diary, MI*[3], I; O'Conor, p. 59). Tradition tells

us both men were called "Fire-men"—a play upon their names deriving from *ignis*—but this is not wholly correct. The Emperor Severus called Ignatius of Antioch "the fiery one," because he burned with the "glow of divine love"; Romanos in a hymn to the Saint styled him the *"Pyrpoloumenos,"* that is, "one who fights with fire." Ignatius of Loyola sent out his *Compagna* with these words: "Ite omnia incendite et inflammate." (Bartoli, *Vita Ignatii,* IV, 14.)

[110] *Trallians,* V, 2 (p. 76).

[111] *Philadelphians,* VII, 2 (pp. 87–88); *Romans,* VII, 2 (p. 83).

[112] *Trallians,* IV, 2 (p. 76). Here is explicit reference to the "discretion of urging love" (*caritas Christi urget nos*), by means of which the battle of Satan is characterized: "What I need is equanimity (discreet moderation), by which the Prince of this world is undone." *Trallians,* V, 1 (p. 76), measures the genuineness of mystical knowledge almost entirely by its usefulness in pastoral care.

[113] *Smyrnaeans,* VI, 2 (p. 92).

[114] *Romans,* VI, 3 (p. 83).

[115] *Ephesians,* X, 3 (p. 64).

[116] *Philadelphians,* III, 1 (p. 86).

[117] *Ephesians,* V, 3 (p. 62).

[118] *Trallians,* XI, 1–2 (p. 78).

[119] *Philadelphians,* VII, 1–2 (pp. 87–88).

[120] *Ephesians,* XX, 1–2 (pp. 67–68).

[121] *Ephesians,* XIII (p. 65).

[122] *Ephesians,* XVII, 1 (p. 66).

[123] *Mysticism and Obedience to the Church According to Ignatius Loyola, MI⁴, I, 305–306 and 407; II, 76; MI¹, I, 105; XII, 632 ff.*

[124] *Polycarp,* VI, 1–2 (p. 98).

[125] *Ephesians,* XIX, 3 (p. 67).

[126] Cf. note 103 above. We find the saying "My Love is crucified" also in the Directory of Father Aegidius Gonzales (*MI²*, I, 933), used there in connection with the devotion to the Sacred Heart cultivated even in the earliest days of the Society.

[127] *Flos Sanctorum,* 36, "The Life of St. Ignatius, Martyr." Cf. also Ch. Clair, *La Vie de Saint Ignace de Loyola* (Paris, 1891), p. 220. Th. Dombart, "Das Monogramm IHS," *Die Christliche Kunst,* XI (1914–15), 257–269.

[128] Compare with this the essay "Del nombre de Jesús y sellos de San Ignacio," in *Cartas de San Ignacio,* I (Madrid, 1874), 416 ff. Ignatius' constant ejaculation was, *"Ay Jesús"* (*MI⁴*, I, 341, 345, 402). He desired that the houses of his Order should bear the monogram IHS (*MI¹*, II, 326 and 329; Epist. Mixt., II, 87).

[129] Ribadeneira, *De Ratione Instituti Societatis Jesu* (Rome, 1864), p. 49.

[130] *MI³*, I, 275–294. Cf. Hugo Rahner, *Zeitschrift für Aszese und Mystik,* XVII (1942), 69.

[131] *Epistola 223,* 2 (*PG* 32, 824 A–B). Cf. *St. Basil, Letters,* Loeb edition, translated by Roy J. Deferrari, 4 volumes, London, 1926–1934.

[132] Cf. M. Viller and Karl Rahner, *Aszese und Mystik in der Väterzeit* (Freiburg, 1939), pp. 123–133.

[133] Hans Urs von Balthasar, "Metaphysik und Mystik des Evagrius Pontikus," in *Zeitschrift für Aszese und Mystic,* XIV (1939), 31–47. On the incalculable importance of Evagrius in the teaching of the Orient on perfection, see Viller-Rahner, *Aszese und Mystik in der Väterzeit,* pp. 108 ff.

[134] *Homily on Psalm 28,* 3 (*PG* 29, 288 B). Cf. B. Jackson, *A Select Library of Nicene and Post-Nicene Fathers of the Christian Church,* Vol. 8, series 2, New York, 1895.

[135] *On the Holy Spirit,* XVI, 39 (*PG* 32, 140 f.; Jackson, *Nicene and Post-Nicene Fathers*).

[136] *On the Holy Spirit,* VIII, 18 (*PG* 32, 100 A–B).

[137] *Letter 261,* 2 (*PG* 32, 969 B; Loeb edition, Vol. 3).

[138] *Letter 243,* 1 (*PG* 32, 904 A; Loeb edition, Vol. 3).

[139] "The Long Rules, Question 7, 2" (*PG* 31, 929 f.; Sister M. M. Wagner, *Saint Basil Ascetical Works,* New York, 1950, *The Fathers of the Church,* pp. 247–252).

[140] "The Long Rules, Question 43, 1, 2" (*PG* 31, 1028 BC; Wagner, *Saint Basil,* pp. 318–320).

[141] "The Long Rules, Question 28, 2" (*PG* 31, 989 B; Wagner, pp. 289–291).—"The Shorter Rules, Question 116" (*PG,* 31, 1161 B; W. K. L. Clarke, *The Ascetic Works of Saint Basil,* New York, 1925, p. 273).

[142] "The Long Rules, Question 26" (*PG* 31, 985 D; Wagner, pp. 288–289).

[143] "The Long Rules, Question 17, 1, 2" (*PG* 31, 961 f.; Wagner, pp. 271–273).

[144] "The Long Rules, Question 19, 1" (*PG* 31, 968 B; Wagner, pp. 275–277). Discretion in the amount and kind of bodily penances taken up. In Greek this *"discretio"* means *"oikonomia,"* that is, "prudent previous calculation and provident distribution." "The Shorter Rules, Question 139" (*PG* 31, 1176 A; Clarke, p. 281) answers the same question briefly. Here "discretion" in Greek means *"logos oikeios tes eusebeias,"* that is, "a reasonableness, working in our interior, which comes from our intimate union with God." For use of the discerning of spirits in time of prayer and work see "The Long Rules, Question 37, 1–2," (*PG* 31, 1009 ff.; Wagner, pp. 306–311). For its use during times of consolation and desolation see "The Shorter Rules, Question 16," (*PG* 31, 1092 f.; Clarke, p. 236).

[145] Cf. also *Letter 139,* 1 (*PG* 32, 581 C; Loeb edition, Vol. 2, pp. 325–331); *Letter 45,* 2 (*PG* 32, 368 B; Loeb, Vol. 2, pp. 23–27).

[146] "An Introduction to the Ascetical Life" (*PG* 31, 620 f.; Wagner, pp. 9–13).

[147] "Long Rules, Question 20, 2" (*PG* 31, 1080 A; Wagner, pp. 277–280).

[148] *Letter 277, 1* (*PG* 32, 1013 A; Loeb, Vol. 3).

[149] *AB,* XCVIII (O'Conor, p. 141). Cf. Hugo Rahner, "From Montserrat to St. Paul: the Relation Between Benedict and Ignatius," in *Maria Einsiedeln,* a Benedictine monthly magazine, November, 1941.

[150] *MI³,* I, cxc ff., and ccxii ff. See also *Zeitschrift für Aszese und Mystik,* XVII (1942), 69.

[151] H. G. Mallinckrodt, "Die Stellung des Abtes in der Regel des hl. Benedict und die alte Bischofsidee bei Ignatius von Antiochien," in *Liturgische Zeitschrift,* II (1930), 14–20.

[152] *Rule 73* (*PL* 66, 930 A; *The Holy Rule of St. Benedict,* St. Meinrad, Indiana, 1937, p. 109). Here St. Benedict states expressly that the Rule of St. Basil is a guide to the highest perfection. See also St. Hilpisch, "Die Quellen zum Charakterbild des hl. Benedikt," in *Zeitschrift für katholische Theologie,* XLIX (1925), 365.

[153] *Rule 1* (*PL* 66, 246 B; St. Meinrad edition, p. 12).

[154] Cf. the excellent summary in St. Hilpisch, *loc. cit.,* p. 369: "Free monasticism, led by the spirit alone, is replaced by rule-bound monasticism. Pachomius, although he regulated all external details of monastic life, left free choice in the ascetical life. Not so, however, St. Benedict: for him, the Rule is the norm and next to it the Abbot, to whom all teaching and authority belongs. The strict enforcement of this principle everywhere prepares the way for a new type of monasticism."

[155] *Rule 7* (*PL* 66, 373 A; St. Meinrad edition, pp. 26–34). This text is cited by Benedict as coming from Holy Scripture, but is actually taken from the Acts of the Martyrs of Saints Agape and Chionia. The words are: *"Voluntas poenam habet, necessitas parit coronam."*

[156] *Rule, Prologue* (*PL* 66, 218 C; St. Meinrad edition, pp. 7–11). "We have, therefore, to establish a school of the Lord's

service . . . and if we wish to dwell in the tabernacle of His kingdom, we can never attain to it unless we run thither by the practice of good works."

[157] *Rule, Prologue* (*PL* 66, 218 D; St. Meinrad edition, pp. 7–11).

[158] *Ibid.* (*PL* 66, 215 D; St. Meinrad, p. 8).

[159] Cf. E. von Hippel, *Die Krieger Gottes, Die Regel Benedikts als Ausdruck frühchristlicher Gemeinschaftsbildung* (Halle, 1936).

[160] *Rule, Prologue* (*PL* 66, 218 B; St. Meinrad edition, p. 11). "Therefore, our hearts and our bodies must be prepared to fight under holy obedience to His commands."

[161] Cf. St. Hilpisch, *Zeitschrift für katholische Theologie,* XLIX (1925), 372–375, where the particular details of Benedictine "discretion," as against those of ancient monasticism, are well summed up.

[162] *Dialogi, II,* 36 (*PL* 66, 200 D). "Discretione praecipua, sermone luculenta."

[163] *Rule, Prologue* (*PL* 66, 218 C; St. Meinrad edition, p. 11).

[164] *Rule 73* (*PL* 66, 929 f.; St. Meinrad edition, p. 109).

[165] Cf. Nicolas Orlandini, *Historia Societatis Jesu* (Coloniae, 1621), I, 38 ff.

[166] *MH Nadal,* IV, 651 ff.

[167] Gregory the Great, *Dialogi,* II, 35 (*PL* 66, 200 AB).

[168] St. Augustine, *Confessions, V,* 9 (*PL* 32, 713 C). From the Manichaean viewpoint, he considers "the death of the flesh of Christ senseless"; V, 10 (*PL* 32, 715 B); "he doubts whether the truth of the Eternal God should be enclosed in the Church"; VII, 9 (*PL* 32, 740 f.): he describes from a Platonic standpoint his failure to understand the humility, cross, and death of the man Jesus.

[169] Sermon 339, 4 (G. Morin, *Sermones S. Augustini post*

Maurinos reperti, Romae, 1930, p. 193). Cf. also F. Hofmann, *Der Kirchenbegriff des hl. Augustinus* (München, 1933), pp. 76–77. See H. Urs von Balthasar, *Augustinus, Das Antlitz der Kirche* (Einsiedeln, 1942).

[170] *MI*³, II, ccvi f., 64.—Cf. *Zeitschrift für Aszese und Mystik,* XVII (1942), 69 f.

[171] *Adventuale de inspirationibus, Sermon 2 (Opera Omnia,* Venice, 1745, III, 138 B).

[172] Wessel Gransfort, who died in 1489, was a disciple of the Brothers of the Common Life. For his ascetical doctrine and his influence on Luther, see Nicolaus Paulus in *Katholik,* II (1900), 11, 138, 226–228.

[173] Cf. C. A. Kneller, *Zeitschrift für katholische Theologie,* Vol. 49 (1925), 170 ff.

[174] Gerson, *De distinctione verarum visionum a falsis (Opera Omnia,* Antwerp, 1706), I, 44–45.

[175] *To the Magnesians,* V (Kleist, p. 70).

[176] Cassian, *Collationes* I, 20 (*PL* 49, 510 B). Here is found an indication of the ancient use of this remarkable saying.

[177] *MI*², I, 927.

[178] *Dialogo,* chap. 72 (edited at Venice, 1611, pp. 228–229). A citation is also taken from C. A. Kneller, *Zeitschrift für katholische Theologie,* XLIX (1925), 178. Cf. also the new edition of her letters, *Katharina von Siena, Politische Briefe,* translated by Ferdinand Strobel (Einsiedeln, 1945).

[179] *De praxi divinae praesentiae* XXI, 13 (Cracow edition, 1889, p. 346).

[180] Cf. also his series of sermons, *De pugna spirituali (Opera Omnia,* Venice, 1745, III, 69–113). On p. 78 he mentions the "Babylonian camp"; on p. 80 he speaks of the peasant and the noble in battle, that is, of the ordinary man and the knight in the service of Christ; on p. 83 he describes the Church as *"acies ordinata";* on p. 80 he says Christ the

King is the *"Capitaneus Ecclesiae."* See also his sermon, *De exercitu spirituum malignorum* (III, 407–413).

[181] In his *Sermon 2,* on *Adventuale de inspirationibus* (*Opera Omnia,* III, 125–139).

[182] *MI*[1], I, 505. An English translation of the letter to the scholastics of Coimbra appears in *Renovation Reading* (Woodstock College, 1931), pp. 11–22. The text cited here by St. Ignatius is from Pseudo-Bernard, *De vita solitaria* (*PL* 184, 238 C): *"Omnibus in rebus res est discretio summa."*

[183] *MI*[4], I, 219–220.

[184] Bernardine of Siena, *Opera,* III, 134 AB.

[185] Thus he is called by Enea Silvio de' Piccolomini, later Pope Pius II. Cf. Pastor, *History of the Popes* (Freiburg, 1901), I, 37.

[186] *Ibid.,* Vol. 1.

[187] *MH Chron. Pol.,* I, 72–73.

[188] Text from the "Summario Castellano" of Father Polanco, of 1548, which has not been completely published as yet. Excerpts have been published in Leturia's "Genesis de los Ejercicios," p. 53. Now in the *MH Fontes Narrativi* (Rome, 1943), I, 185.

[189] *MI*[4], II, 75. The whole text in a German translation by Hugo Rahner appears in *Zeitschrift für Aszese und Mystik,* X (1935), 135.

[190] Ribadeneira, *Vita Ignatii Loyolae,* I, 13 (Coloniae, 1602), pp. 83 ff. See also *MI*[1], V, 95.

[191] *MH Chron. Pol.,* III, 24. Cf. *MI*[1], IV, 106 and 309.

[192] *MI*[3], I, 26.

[193] *MI*[2], I, 218 and 150. *Directorium,* 1599, prooemium 2, *MI*[2], I, 1116.

[194] *AB,* XXIX (O'Conor, p. 56).

[195] *AB,* XXX (O'Conor, p. 57). Cf. *MI*[4], I, 473 and 337, where Ignatius states that all the teachers the world has known could not have the influence God had on his mind at Manresa.

[196] *MH Chron. Pol.,* III, 530.

[197] *MI*[2], I, 216.

[198] *MI*[2], I, 663.

[199] *MI*[2], I, 667.

[200] *Constitutiones,* IV, 8, 5; *MI*[3], III, 133.

[201] This is the statement of Polanco in his Preface to the Vulgate edition of the Exercises, *MI*[2], I, 218. The same was said by the anonymous writer of the Directory, *MI*[2], I, 883.

[202] *MI*[2], I, 666. Cf. *ibid.,* pp. 846, 898, 972, 1126.

[203] *MI*[2], I, 667. This knowledge served Dr. Torres well when he was elevated from his professorship to the episcopacy. As one source whimsically puts it, *"a pulvere scholastico in praesulem translatus,"* "He was lifted from the classroom's dust to the bishop's palace." (*MI*[2], I, 574.)

[204] *MI*[2], I, 883.

[205] *MH Nadal,* IV, p. 678.

[206] *MI*[2], I, 949.

[207] *MI*[2], I, 933. Cf. P. Sinthern, "Die Direcktorien zum Exerzitienbüchlein, ihre Geschichte und ihr Inhalt," in *Studien zu den Exerzitien des hlgen Ignatius von Loyola* (Innsbruck, 1925), I, 71 ff.

[208] Father Fabius de Fabiis especially adverts to this point in his Directory, with particular reference to the theology of sin in the First Week. "With regard to the meditations on sin and likewise in the other fundamental questions which are laid down in the Spiritual Exercises, it is certainly not sufficient merely to give the bare wording and an approximate meaning of the text, but a deep knowledge and diligent

study is needed." (*MI²*, I, 947.) Cf. also the insistent warning of the learned Dr. Ortiz, who made the Exercises under Ignatius at Monte Cassino in 1538, against theological dilettantism in regard to the Exercises (*MI²*, I, 699 f.).

209 Cf. *MI¹*, I, 278, note 3.

210 Cf. the description of primitive Christian theology on this renunciation of the devil and the promise of adherence to Christ, by Hugo Rahner in "Pompa diaboli," *Zeitschrift für katholische Theologie,* LV (1931), 239–273.

211 *MI²*, I, 861: "Notandum quod contemplatio de Rege . . . est velut fundamentum omnium meditationum vitae Domini N. Jesu Chr."

212 This incorporation is true at any rate for the final redaction of the text, however much the content itself, according to Ignatius' own testimony, is a part of the original draft of the Exercises based on his own experience (*AB*, IX and XCIX; O'Conor, pp. 27 and 122). We may cite as an example the quotation from St. Thomas (I–II, q. 9, a. 1; q. 10, a. 4) which Ignatius added to the second rule for the discernment of spirits for the Second Week, in the *Versio Prima, MI²*, I, 529, 49, note 1. For the theological tradition of the first rule of the Second Week, cf. *MI²*, I, 89, note 1. The cautious Father Kneller holds that an influence of the *Dialogo* of St. Catherine of Siena cannot be altogether excluded: *Zeitschrift für katholische Theologie,* XLIX (1925), 183.

213 *MI²*, I, 779 and 781 f.

214 *De Religione Societatis Jesu,* IX, 5, 30–41 (*Opera Omnia,* Paris, 1857, XVI, 1028–1033).

215 Jac. Alvarez de Paz, *De inquisitione pacis sive studio orationis,* V, 4 (*Opera Omnia,* Paris, 1876, VI, 624–677).

216 J. B. Scaramelli, *Discernimento de' Spiriti* (Venice, 1753). In the German edition (*Die Unterscheidung der Geister,* Ratisbonne, 1888), there is an extract from Cardinal John Bona's *De discretione spirituum* (*Opera,* Antwerp, 1739). Both of these works provide an insight into the patristic and scholastic tradition in regard to the discernment of spirits.

[217] Father Leturia recently treated this question in his "Genesis de los Ejercicios," pp. 29–31. A number of authors have already studied it at length; cf. Dudon-Young, *St. Ignatius of Loyola,* Appendix VI, pp. 452–455. J. Criexell, "Explication de una cuestion hagiografica," *Razon y Fe,* XX (1908), 217 ff. Father Van Ortroy, "Manrèse et les origines de la Compagnie de Jésus," *Analecta bollandiana,* XXVII (1908), 393–418. Hugo Rahner in *Zeitschrift für Aszese und Mystik,* X (1935), 273 ff. Huonder, *Ignatius,* pp. 65–70.

[218] *AB,* L (O'Conor, p. 80).

[219] *AB,* LXX (O'Conor, p. 108).

[220] Cf. *MI*[1], I, 199 (Letter of July, 1537): "What God's designs are in regard to my future life, I do not know." The plan of founding a "Company" was first concretely envisaged in the deliberations held during the Lent of 1539. (Text in *MI*[3], I, 1–14.) Cf. Hugo Rahner, "From Montmartre to St. Paul," in *Mitteilungen* of the German Province, CIII (1935), 389–398. Leturia, "Importancia del año 1538 en el cumplimiento del voto de Montmartre," in *Archivum historicum Societatis Jesu,* IX (1940), 188–207.

[221] *AB,* XLV (O'Conor, p. 73): ". . . his purpose of helping others save their souls" in Jerusalem. *AB,* L (O'Conor, p. 80): ". . . to study in order to be better fitted to save souls." *AB,* LIV (O'Conor, p. 85): ". . . at Manresa, there was a holy monk . . . with whom Ignatius wished to remain, as well for his own personal guidance as to prepare himself to direct others."

[222] *MH* Ribadeneira, II, 903 f.

[223] Published by Father Leturia, "Genesis de los Ejercicios," pp. 56–57.

[224] *MI*[4], I, 220.

[225] *MH Nadal,* IV, 652.

[226] A. Astrain, *Historia de la Compañia de Jesus* (Madrid, 1902), I, 106, note 1.

[227] Leturia, "Genesis de los Ejercicios," p. 56.

[228] *Ibid.,* p. 30, note 53.

[229] Sacchini in the Preface to *Historia Societatis Jesu* by Nicolas Orlandini (Cologne, 1621), p. 2.

[230] N. Orlandini, *Historia Societatis Jesu,* p. 28.

[231] Cf. Hugo Rahner, *Zeitschrift für Aszese und Mystik,* X (1935), 273 f.

[232] *Camino espiritual,* Book V, Chapter 2 (Madrid, 1860, II, 301).

[233] *De praestantia Instituti Societatis Jesu* (published at Cracow, 1890), pp. 12 f. Cf. Father Van Ortroy, *Manrèse et les origines de la Compagnie de Jésus,* p. 413.

[234] Oliver Manare, *De vita et moribus Everardi Mercuriani* (Brussels, 1882), pp. 77–87; Appendix: *Exhortationes Mercuriani.*

[235] Cf. Hugo Rahner, *Zeitschrift für Aszese und Mystik,* X (1935), 127–129.

[236] *Spiritual Diary, MI*[3], I, 104.

[237] Suarez, *De Religione Societatis Jesu,* I, 2, no. 10 (*Opera Omnia,* Paris, 1860, XVI, 565).

[238] *MI*[1], IV, 671 (in the "Letter on Obedience").

[239] E. Przywara, "Deus semper major," *Theologie der Exerzitien,* (Freiburg, 1940), III, 337.

[240] *Directorium,* I, 8 (*MI*[2], I, 799).

[241] *To the Trallians,* IX, 1 (Kleist, p. 77).

[242] The formulation of the Jesuit way of life as that of an *"honestus sacerdos"* originates from Ignatius himself. This expression is an explicit addition to the Formula *"Quicumque."* It is found for the first time in the Bull of Julius III, *Exposcit debitum,* of 1550; the wording is *"Honestorum sacerdotum communem et approbatum usum sequantur."*

The expression is not found in the first draft of the Formula found in the Bull *Regimini* of 1540. *Institutum Societatis Jesu* (Florence, 1892), I, 26.

[243] Suarez, *De Religione Societatis Jesu,* Preface and Chapter 1 (XVI, 554–560).

[244] *Ibid.,* I, 13 (p. 560).

[245] *Examen Generale,* IV, 44–45 (*MI³*, III, 29).

[246] *MH Nadal,* IV, 678.

[247] *Spiritual Diary, MI³*, I, 131: "Dadme humildad amorosa y asi de reverencia y acatamiento."

[248] *MI²*, I, 789.

Bibliography

A Short Bibliography to Aid in the
Study of Ignatian Spirituality

ASTRAIN, A., *Historia de la Compañia de Jesús en la Asistencia de España*, I, Madrid, 2nd edition, 1912.

BERNARD, H., "Essai historique sur les Exercices de saint Ignace," Louvain, *Museum Lessianum*, 1926.

BOHMER, H., *Loyola und die deutsche Mystik*, Leipsig, 1921.

————, *Studien zur Geschichte der Gesellschaft Jesu*, I, Bonn, 1914.

BROU, A., *Ignatian Methods of Prayer*, translated by William J. Young, Milwaukee, 1949.

————, *The Ignatian Way to God*, translated by William J. Young, Milwaukee, 1951.

BRUCKER, J., "Ignace de Loyola," *Dictionnaire de théologie catholique*, VII, 1921.

CHASTONAY, P. DE, "Des Abtes Cisneros Geistliche Übungen," *Stimmen der Zeit*, XCVI (1918), 497–506.

CODINA, A., "De fontibus externis libri Exercitiorum," *Mon. Ignatiana*, II, 1, Madrid, 1919, pp. 47–136.

————, *Los origenes de los Ejercicios espirituales de san Ignacio de Loyola*, Barcelona, 1926.

————, "San Ignasi a Montserrat," Rome, *Archivum historicum Societatis Jesu,* VII, 1938.

Directory to the Spiritual Exercises of Our Holy Father Ignatius, Authorized Translation, London, 1925.

DUDON, P., *St. Ignatius of Loyola,* translated by William J. Young, Milwaukee, 1949.

GILL, H. V., *Jesuit Spirituality,* Dublin, 1935.

GOODIER, A., *St. Ignatius Loyola and Prayer,* New York, 1940.

GRANDMAISON, L. DE, "Les Exercices de saint Ignace," *Monumenta Rech. Sc. Rel.,* X (1920), 391–408.

HUONDER, A., *Ignatius von Loyola, Beiträge zu seinem Charakterbild,* Cologne, 1932.

KNELLER, C. A., "Zu den Kontroversen über den hl. Ignatius von Loyola Quellen der Exerzitien," *Zeitschrift für katholische Theologie,* XLIX (1925), 161–185.

KREITEN, W., "Zur Entstehung des Exerzitienbüchleins," *Stimmen aus Maria Laach,* XXIII (1882), 32–55, 154–171.

LETURIA, P., *El gentilhombre Iñigo López de Loyola en su patria y en su siglio,* Montevideo, 1938 (2nd edition, Barcelona, 1949). The English translation by Aloysius J. Owen, is entitled *Iñigo de Loyola* (Syracuse, N. Y., 1949).

————, "Génesis de los Ejercicios de san Ignacio y su influjo en la fundación de la Compañía de Jesús," *Archivum historicum Societatis Jesu,* X (1941), 16–59.

————, "La conversión de san Ignacio: nuevos datos y ensayo de síntesis," *Archivum historicum Societatis Jesu,* V (1936), 1–35.

————, "El Reino de Cristo y los prólogos del Flos Sanctorum de Loyola," *Manresa,* IV (1928), 334–349.

————, "El influjo de san Onofre en san Ignacio a base de un texto inédito de Nadal," *Manresa,* II (1926), 224–238.

————, "La 'devotio moderna' en el Montserrat de san Ignacio," *Razón y Fe,* CXI (1936), 371–386.

MESCHLER, M., *The Spiritual Exercises of St. Ignatius,* Woodstock College, 1899.

O'CONOR, J., *The Autobiography of St. Ignatius,* New York, 1900.

PINARD DE LA BOULLAYE, H., *Les étapes de rédaction des Exercices de saint Ignace,* Paris, 1945.

POLIT, M. ESPINOSA, *Perfect Obedience,* Westminster, Maryland, 1947.

PUHL, L., *The Spiritual Exercises of St. Ignatius, A New Translation,* Westminster, Maryland, 1951.

RAHNER, H., "Ignatius von Loyola und die aszetische Tradition der Kirchenväter," *Zeitschrift für Aszese und Mystik,* XVII (1942), 61–77.

————, "Die Vision des heiligen Ignatius in der Kapelle von La Storta. Ein Beitrag zur Geschichte und Psychologie der ignatianischen Mystik," *Zeitschrift für Aszese und Mystik,* X (1935), 17–35, 124–139, 202–220, 265–282.

————, *Ignatius von Loyola. Geistliche Briefe,* Einsiedeln, 1942.

————, "Ignatius der Beichtvater," *Anima,* I (1947), 375–384.

————, "Die Grabschrift des Loyola," *Stimmen der Zeit,* LXII (1947), 321–337.

ROHR, E., "Franziskus und Ignatius. Eine vergleichende Studie," *Zur religiösen Lage der Gegenwart,* XIV (1926), 1–84.

SUSTA, J., "'Ignatius' von Loyola Selbstbiographie. Eine quellengeschichliche Studie," *Mittellungen des Instituts für österreichische Geschichtsforschung,* XXVI (1905), 45–106.

TEIXIDOR, L., "San Agustin y los Ejercicios," *Manresa,* VI (1930), 337–364.

TOURNIER, F., "Les deux Cités dans la littérature chrétienne," *Etudes,* CXXIII (1910), 644–665.

VAN ORTROY, F., "Manrèse et les origines de la Compagnie de Jésus," *Analecta Bollandiana,* XXVII (1908), 393–418.

WATRIGANT, H., *La genèse des Exercises de saint Ignace,* Amiens, 1897.

ZANNKE, L., *Die Exercitia spiritualia des Ignatius von Loyola in ihren geistesgeschichtlichen Zusammenhangen,* Leipzig, 1931.

ZEIGER, J., "Gefolgschaft des Hernn. Ein rechtsgeschichtlicher Beitrag zu den Exerzitien des hl. Ignatius," *Zeitschrift für Aszese und Mystik,* XVII (1942), pp. 1–16.

Index